PARRAKEETS OF THE WORLD

DR. MATTHEW M. VRIENDS

PICTORIAL CREDITS

Front and back covers: FRITZ PRENZEL.

Color: DR. G. ALLEN: 136 (1), 141 (2), 156, 157, 216 (2), 217, 289 (4). DR. HERBERT R. AXELROD: 48, 53, 96, 105 (3), 116, 117, 124, 128, 137, 177, 211, 221, 257, 297 (5), 308, 312, 313, 317. J. CHELMAN AND D. PETRULLA: 160 (2), 161 (3), 180, 181, 196, 265, 304, 305, 309 (2), 316 (2). K. DONNELLY: 164, 165. KEITH HINDWOOD: 168, 169. J. M. KENNING: 41. PAUL KWAST: 36 (2). HARRY V. LACEY: 37 (4, 5), 68, 119, 125. A.J. MOBBS: 73 (1), 121, 256. IRENE AND MICHAEL MOROCOMBE: 129, 153, 205, 260, 261, 320. HORST MUELLER (VOGELPARK WALSRODE): 37 (2), 56 (2), 60, 64, 65, 69, 77, 88, 89, 105 (2), 112 (1, 2), 113 (4,5), 120, 136 (2, 3), 141 (3, 4, 5, 6), 145, 152, 184 (1), 185, 208, 212 (2), 216 (1), 233, 268, 281 (3), 285 (2), 293 (3), 296 (1, 2), 297 (4), 300, 301, 316 (1). AARON NORMAN: 225, 276. FRITZ PRENZEL: 188, 189, 244, 277. L. ROBINSON: 284. SAN DIEGO ZOO: 44, 45, 72, 73 (1), 92, 93, 108, 109, 132, 133, 160, 161 (4), 192, 193, 209, 220, 232, 236, 237, 248, 249, 252, 264, 288, 289 (3), 292. DR. MATTHEW M. VRIENDS AND P. LEYSEN: 36 (1), 40, 52, 57, 61, 76, 85, 97, 100, 101, 112 (3), 144, 148, 149, 172, 173, 184 (2), 197, 200, 201, 212 (1), 224, 229, 241, 245, 253, 269, 280, 281 (4), 285 (2), 293 (4), 296 (3), 309 (3).

Black and white: DR. G. ALLEN: 14, 20, 110 (2), 182, 183. DR. HERBERT R. AXELROD: 27 (5), 62 (1), 87 (3), 255 (5), 341 (6, 7). K. DONNELLY: 39 (3), 42 (2), 63 (5). HARRY V. LACEY: 1, 9, 39 (1), 43, 47, 54, 74, 78, 194 (1), 195, 223 (4, 5), 238, 270 (1, 3), 282, 328 (2), 329, 334 (2), 335 (5), 340 (1), 341 (4, 5), 360. LOUISE VAN DER MEID: 26, 27 (3, 4), 31, 42 (1), 62 (2), 75 (2, 4), 79, 87 (4), 94, 95, 103, 111, 122 (1), 123 (3), 223 (6), 239, 254, 255 (3, 4), 271 (4), 283, 323 (2, 3), 334 (1), 340 (2, 3), 346, 347. FRED B. MUDDITT: 271, (5), 328 (1). HORST MUELLER: 75 (3), 183 (5, 6), 194 (2, 3), 323 (1), 334 (3), 335 (4). CARL NAETHER: 122 (2), 222 (3). J. CHELMAN AND D. PETRULLA: 123 (4). JOHN WARHAM: 222 (1, 2), 270 (3).

ISBN 0-87666-999-2

© 1979 by T.F.H. Publications, Inc., Ltd.

Distributed in the U.S. by T.F.H. Publications, Inc., 211 West Sylvania Avenue, P.O. Box 427, Neptune, N.J. 07753; in England by T.F.H. (Gt. Britain) Ltd., 13 Nutley Lane, Reigate, Surrey; in Canada to the book store and library trade by Beaverbooks, 953 Dillingham Road, Pickering, Ontario L1W 1Z7; in Canada to the pet trade by Rolf C. Hagen Ltd., 3225 Sartelon Street, Montreal 382, Quebec; in Southeast Asia by Y.W. Ong, 9 Lorong 36 Geylang, Singapore 14; in Australia and the South Pacific by Pet Imports Pty. Ltd., P.O. Box 149, Brookvale 2100, N.S.W., Australia; in South Africa by Valiant Publishers (Pty.) Ltd., P.O. Box 78236, Sandton City, 2146, South Africa; Published by T.F.H. Publications, Inc., Ltd., The British Crown Colony of Hong Kong.

Contents

3

4

"Soyons fidèles à nos faiblesses"
for my daughter Tanya

PREFACE

Peach-fronted conure, *Aratinga aurea* — a charming bird both in the wild and in the aviary. The species of the genus *Aratinga* range from Mexico to South America.

The keeping, breeding, and care of parrakeets or small parrots is still a fairly new branch in the bird fancier's world, no doubt due to the high prices of these particular birds. In addition, there is currently very little responsible literature available on this subject—and of course it is a risky business to simply buy birds, place them in a cage or aviary, and hope for the best when one does not know how to take proper care of them.

It has been my privilege to compile this book on the most common parrakeets that are kept in captivity today. Many little known and even very rare species have been given some attention as well, just for the sake of completeness. The scope of this book has been limited to parrakeets, and much of it is devoted to the so-called rosellas and the other Australian parrakeets, composed of 36 species, even though a few works have recently been published on these particular species. Many interesting factors came to light during my three-year stay in Australia, and of course these have been included in this book.

As used here, parrakeet is almost synonymous with small parrots from South America, Asia, and Australia. American readers should not confuse these with the budgie or parakeet. Although from a scientific viewpoint the well known budgerigar (*Melopsittacus undulatus*) belongs in the group of rosellas, I have left these birds out for the simple reason that there are numerous books available on this bird alone, including *Breeding Budgerigars* (T.F.H. Publications, Neptune, N.J.), which I recommend to the interested reader. I have also covered the particulars concerning the cockatiel (*Nymphicus hollandicus*), although this bird is correctly considered by ornithologists to fall somewhere between the rosellas and the cockatoos. In spite of this, I felt it would be wise to include information on this particular bird, so frequently the choice of bird fanciers.

It should speak for itself that I will cover the most well known species in the greatest detail, making use of experiences gained by both local and foreign breeders. I am very pleased that I had the opportunity to freely work on the outline of this book while in Australia. The final format, however, was drawn up in the United States with the cooperation of some outstanding ornithologists and the use of the library at the University of Florida at Gainesville, while my students also assisted me with the compilation of data both national and international. After researching their information and placing it in its proper perspective, it proved to be extremely worthwhile. It is interesting to note that many of these students not only kept various species of parrakeets in their gardens and apartments to see how they would react to captivity and other stimuli and to study their behavior, but many of these students are currently enthusiastic aviculturists.

Everyone can keep, breed, and take care of parrakeets. Not all of them are expensive, nor do they all require involved care. Since this book is written with the intention of giving as much instructional information as possible, I would regard it as suitable for both the beginner and the advanced bird fancier and breeder. The people of the Netherlands and Belgium have always been interested in parrots and parrakeets. In the preface of an earlier book, *Het Nieuwe Volièreboek,* published by Elsevier in Amsterdam and Brussels, I spoke in great detail about the countless sailors and sea captains who brought home to their wives, sweethearts, or political connections one or more colorful hook-beaked birds obtained during their voyages for the East Indies Company in 1602. It is obvious from old literature on parrots and parrakeets that back in 1400 these birds were already being kept in cages and aviaries both in the Netherlands and other parts of Europe, but all too often, unfortunately, without much success! After 1600, however, we find that some very rare species were being kept in very well cared for aviaries. Wealthy people, in fact, employed a special attendant whose job was to take care of the birds and perhaps any other animals they might keep. In most cases these attendants were from the East Indies and received high salaries because some bird collections were worth astronomical amounts of money.

It is apparent that parrakeets and parrots have been kept in captivity by man over the centuries, as also evidenced in the writings of Aristotle. The parrots he refers to came to Greece via the East Indies, having been brought back with the retreating armies of Alexander the Great. Parrots and parrakeets were kept not only for their colorful beauty . . . they were also kept for consumption. The tongues and heads in particular were considered a delicacy. The infamous and wasteful Roman Heliogabalus went down in history as the man who fed parrot heads to his lions and even treated his guests with an extra course of festively prepared parrot heads from time to time! Alexander the Great's famous general, Onesikrit, came across tamed parrakeets kept by various East Indies tribes. According to the works of the biologist and philosopher Plinius, these tamed parrakeets must have been the commonly held rose-ringed parrakeet (*Psittacula krameri manillensis*).

We can conclude from this that parrots and parrakeets have fascinated man for a very long time indeed. Didn't the Inca Indians pay their taxes with the colorful feathers of the scarlet macaw (*Ara macao*)? According to one of the companions of Christopher Columbus, namely the learned scholar Pinzou, the very discovery of America was helped along by a troop of parrots (parrakeets?) that flew in a southwesterly direction over the little fleet in the evening, from which it was surmised that they must be seeking land for the night (although this is a story that most likely should be taken with a grain of salt!). On another occasion, in 1509, the parrots and parrakeets of the village of Yurbaco on the Isthmus of Panama saved the inhabitants of the village by their loud alarmed screaming on the verge of an attack by the infamous Spaniards Hojeda and Nicusesa. Due to the birds' screaming, the inhabitants had just enough time to flee into the jungles so they did not fall into the hands of those murderous bands.

After 1545, when the sea passage along the Cape of Good Hope was discovered and the Indies and Australia (also called "Parrotland") were opened to explorers, more and more different species became known. Although much data was still missing and it was far from complete, a simple guide book written by Aldrovandi was available in 1599. His work included 14 species! Not until many years later did the expensive books covering the works of Levaillan and Elliot become available. Unfortunately, these books are no longer available to the general public and can only be seen in some museums and wealthy libraries, where one may be allowed to leaf through them upon request.

As mentioned before, this book covers only parrakeets and small parrots. Since the larger parrots are not kept as extensively by individuals as parrakeets, I felt it best to utilize all available space for more specifics on our beautiful parrakeets, although, no doubt, some will be missing. A format such as this does not allow for too much specialization or too much detail in description, but I have tried to make this work as complete as possible. Any suggestions regarding deficiencies in the book are welcome; they may become useful in the preparation of a possible second edition.

This book will be useful to both the bird fancier and the professional biologist/ornithologist. That is why special attention has been paid to the scientific names and to the order of the various genera, species, and subspecies. This is probably of little concern to the aviculturist, but I felt it important to adhere to the correct ornithological format, and use the most current common names for the same reason, so that the hobbyist who wishes to specialize in certain species will be assisted in obtaining scientific and foreign literature.

A special word of thanks to my wife, Lucy Vriends-Parent. Her knowledge of the Australian bird world never fails to astound me. She has, consequently, contributed much data that have been worked into the text. It was never too much effort for her to accompany me on the occasional lengthy and therefore tiring excursions into the interiors of Australia and Africa. Without her it would have been impossible to write this book!

I wish to thank the publisher for the pleasant cooperative spirit in which we have worked together, and for the granting of my wishes, including those which were not always modest. A special thanks must go to my assistant, Patricia Schulz, for her cooperation on this project. Last but not least, I am particularly grateful to Mrs. T. Wiedlewsky-Parent for her fine translations and editing. On top of this, she has uncomplainingly typed the manuscript.

Dr. Matthew M. Vriends
Neptune, NJ
Spring 1979

1. Buying Parrakeets

Because the cockatiel is such a popular bird, one can find a wide selection of birds from which to choose a good, healthy one.

Purchasing parrakeets is, to some extent, a matter of hoping for the best. To minimize the risks involved in ending up with a bird that is not healthy or will not breed, there are several things we should look for. In the first place, comparison shopping is a good idea. We should closely observe the housing of the prospective bird. If this gives a well kept and clean impression, we next direct our attention to the bird itself. If it has a generally healthy appearance (clear and bright eyes, shiny and smooth plumage, no dirt on the beak or claws, quick reactions to another bird that may happen to come near him), then we are probably looking at a healthy parrakeet. But we should still remain alert.

Not infrequently some of the more expensive parrakeet species are sold to less experienced bird fanciers, although these birds have already proved to be of little value to the fancier because they will not breed. They look healthy enough and full of life, but once we have them in our own aviary for a while we will find they are simply not suitable for breeding. We have spent our hard-earned money on unwilling specimens, birds that end up with a "travelling" type of existence, going from breeder to breeder and from merchant to unwitting buyer.

What can we do to assure ourselves that we are buying good birds? The merchant cannot always guarantee a specific bird type, although the purchaser will of course ask for "bird papers" that are as detailed as possible. However, these are not always on the level, with the result that even the merchant, despite all his experience, could have been deceived. That is why I would advise merchants to limit their purchasing to young birds. . .and of course the same advice applies to the fancier. Naturally, this "rule" would also apply if we buy from an individual breeder.

I am well aware of the fact that even young birds have their good and bad qualities, but these, after all, have yet to reveal themselves, and no one will need to be blamed should any of the birds prove to be less than satisfactory after a while. If, on the other hand, we buy old birds, we can be sure that nine out of ten of them will not be of any use. This is particularly true of the expensive Australian rosellas, which often come from Germany, Denmark, and France and have changed owners several times. Another disadvantage of older birds is that they are no longer as beautiful in coloring and can therefore be picked up for perhaps less than half their usual price; this might prove to be quite tempting!

One might ask why these old birds are no longer suitable specimens. The answer is simple: the majority of older birds that are offered for sale consist of females that are no longer fertile, sterile males, egg-pecking females, females that do not feed their young once they have come out of the egg, males that bother their mates to death, females that lay eggs but will not hatch them, etc., etc. As you can see, buying old birds is tantamount to buying a pig in a poke! This is why I say we should buy only young birds, and then preferably those whose background with regard to rearing and breeding can be checked.

This is especially important where the Australian types are concerned. We can only obtain specimens bred in Europe, Japan, or this country, because Australia forbids the export of birds. The black market is rather active, however, so that annually many birds that have been reared in the wild are offered for sale; these birds, of course, have their pros and cons also. Specimens from South America also require careful inspection because a deplorable situation exists there, as aptly described by Mr. A. A. Prestwich, in *Avicultural Magazine,* 76(4), 1970:

"I cannot claim any great knowledge of the bird trade as operated at present, but I have vivid recollections of several large consignments of parrots, mainly Roseate Cockatoos, Lovebirds and Ring-necked Parrakeets arriving in a deplorable state, many of the birds being either dead or dying shortly after arriving in England. Perhaps I am prejudiced, but I, for one, can well-believe that for every live South American parrot sold in an American pet shop, 50 have died, for one reason or another. Christopher Weathersbee, after a close study of what he describes as the "Amazon Parrot Raid" has made known some of his findings in *Science News,* 4th January, 1969, and *Peruvian Times,* 21st November, 1969. The following are extracts. Since the lifting of the Parrot Ban in the USA in 1967, it has been quite a fad to own a parrot of some kind. Pet shops have been selling them as a "novelty" as fast as they can obtain them. A buyer for F.W. Woolworth, a chain that does a significant portion of the nation's pet selling, says the demand is such that birds cannot be captured fast enough to satisfy it. The prices range up to $50.00 each, and average between $30.00 and $20.00. Weathersbee says: 'The South American parrots are collected in the forest by Indians, who bring them to the nearest riverbank. There they are purchased for a few cents by buyers who cruise up and down the river until they have a boatload. The survivors of the boatload are sold to the Bogota center or abroad.'

" 'One of the things that has conservationists upset about the parrot trade is that there may be very few survivors. It has been estimated that for every live bird sold in an American pet shop, 50 have died. Many are killed during collection, either by rough handling or in order to reach the coveted young. Many more die in cages waiting for the buyer at the river, and the toll continues after the entrepreneur has acquired his charges. Thus to satisfy a demand for 10,000 pet parrots (in a neighborhood of the number imported in the year) as many as half a million birds may have been destroyed.' "

This paints a horrible and clear picture to which I need not add anything. Before a South American specimen reaches a local pet shop, it would appear he has travelled a veritable road to Calvary. The fact that a specimen has even survived this whole ordeal certainly should count for something, such as a strong constitution, perhaps more favorable circumstances during his particular trip, some very good luck, or a litle of each! When we buy such a bird we should give him the very best of care, providing him with a spotlessly clean, airy, and roomy cage as well as a diet that will help him regain some of the strength he lost during his travels from the jungle.

In the event we limit ourselves to buying only young birds, we will be faced with a problem for which there is no simple solution: namely the business of determining the sexes of the birds. In many species determining the sex when they are young (under one year old) is usually an impossibility. Young males that have not yet finished their last juvenile molt look a lot like old hens, while younger males look much like young females, so it is not a simple matter! This is why we should try to get a written agreement with the bird dealer or individual breeder that will allow us to swap one of our birds should we find that we are not in possession of a true pair. It should go without saying that we never buy two birds from the same nest or from the same parents, as this would promote inbreeding, which could have some very unpleasant results indeed.

Guard against buying too many couples; we must not crowd them. The best method is to house each couple in its own aviary or cage. Combining more couples will generally lead to bickering, and breeding results are seldom achieved.

Keep in mind the following points when buying the birds: they should not be lean in the chest, and certainly the breast bone should not be sticking out; the feathers around the cloaca (vent) must be clean and dry; the plumage should be smooth and shiny, and may even give the impression that it has a wax shine on it (something that actually used to be done by some questionable bird merchants!); the eyes should be clear and bright; each foot should have four toes, which must definitely not be misformed; the bird should have a good balance when it is sitting on a perch; and the legs and feet should have a smooth, not scaly, look. You need not be alarmed if a few feathers, such as some in the tail, are broken or damaged; parrakeets are great climbers and it would not be unusual for them to have thus damaged their feathers in a cage. Once the birds are placed in a roomy cage or aviary, the feathers will replace themselves beautifully during the very next molting. Parrakeets should not be housed in quarters that are too small, since many males will then become sterile, and of course, that does very little to promote your hopes for breeding results!

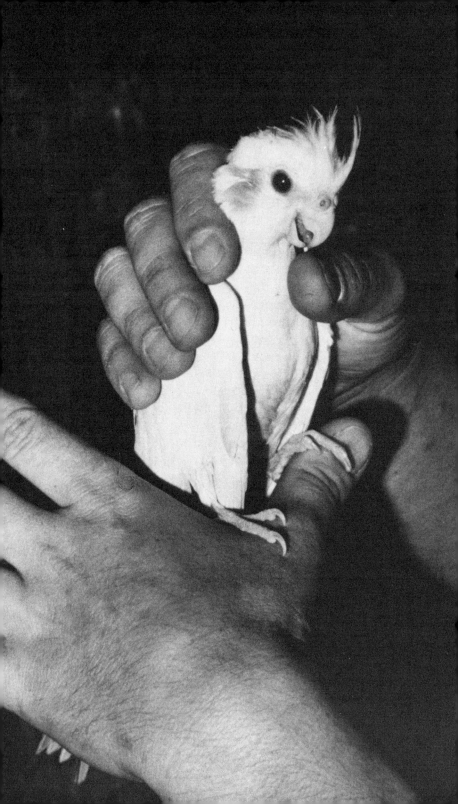

2. Care and Maintenance

Young cockatiel. You should be able to
hold your trained cockatiel in your palm
without having the bird bite you.

Since the majority of the imported parrakeets come from warm and sunny climates, it is very likely that they will have to make some adjustment weatherwise. This is why each new bird should be placed in an individual cage that is cleaned every day; in fact, if once is not enough, then we should do it more often. Cleanliness is absolutely essential here. After cleaning the cage and providing fresh water and food, we should carefully wash our hands with soap to prevent any possible infection from spreading. The cage should be placed in a room that is dry and warm. When we transport a bird during the winter, we should gradually accustom him to the warmth inside and not just place him in a warm area after having been in a colder one. The oxygen in the bones of the bird expands when there is a sudden change to warmth, and not infrequently this causes death of the bird as a result. The temperature where the bird is kept should not drop below 75°-80° F. (26°-28° C.).

We then offer our bird boiled and then cooled water in which we have dissolved a few drops of antibiotics; follow the directions of the veterinarian or those on the label. Above all, do not start playing doctor and changing dosages. Perhaps you feel that a little more antibiotics might speed up the recovery, but the proper amounts of these preparations can do wonders in improving the general health and appearance of your bird while overdoses may be dangerous. Once the parrakeet has become accustomed to its housing and new climate, we will often be amazed by its great ability to adjust. Low temperatures, often below the freezing point, do not faze them. However, no parrot or parrakeet can tolerate a draft, so be especially mindful of them.

Recently imported birds are accustomed to a lot of sunlight and warmth. In order to give them as much sunshine as possible, we could provide them with the light and warmth of a full-spectrum lamp (check with your dealer). Do not use a sunlamp, however; these are injurious to birds' eyes. Obviously, we should only switch the heat lamp on for limited time periods, perhaps three to fifteen minutes a day, starting with three minutes and gradually working up to fifteen. We should place the lamp so that our bird can also sit out of its glow should it so desire. Artificial lighting is also recommended, especially if our birds arrive during the fall or winter. The whole idea is to provide them with daylight as long as possible, allowing them more time to eat and become used to their new environment, not to mention captivity. However, we should not place the cage in direct sunlight; although these birds like warmth and sun, they also need to have shade. On the other hand, it is not sensible to place the cage in a location where no sunlight comes in at all.

When picking up a recently imported bird, the utmost care is advisable. Many of these birds may have been living until very recently in the wild, so that being handled makes them very nervous and frightened. They respond by nipping incessantly—and their beaks are capable of inflicting fairly bad wounds—so be careful and try to remain calm and peaceful under all circumstances. Should your bird escape, remain calm; calling to it and moving around too much just tend to make the bird even more upset, and in that state he can inflict an injury with both beak and claws. When holding him, hold his head securely with one hand while the other hand holds his back in a sturdy grip that includes the wings, pressing them against the bird's flanks; in this way there will not be any nervous wing flapping. A panic-stricken escaped bird should be approached cautiously. Throwing a kitchen towel or other light cloth over the bird will facilitate catching it quickly, cutting out a lot of unnecessary terror for the bird. If your bird arrives in an almost closed cage or container, wear leather gloves when taking it out. Place a firm grip with your right hand on the bird's neck so that he can at most barely move his head. Handling him firmly, but never roughly, should not make your bird nervous . . . or more nervous than he already is. Where possible, you can hold both the opening of the container and the opening of the cage together so the bird can himself travel from container to cage. If there are bars or holes in the container, these should be covered with a handkerchief or other cloth; the bird will then naturally move toward the light of the cage. If necessary, we can always use a stick pushing against his tail to encourage him to take the last step toward better housing and care.

Obviously we should avoid handling our birds as much as possible. Quite often one starts with the taming of a parrakeet by placing him in a separate cage for speech lessons, etc., and then returning him to his regular abode when the school period is over. This is contrary to the very important rule to handle your birds as little as possible. Even when they are very tame and can quote entire litanies, there is no reason to pick them up with your hands. Parrakeets and parrots have good memories, and unpleasant experiences are not soon forgotten. I have known plenty of birds that persistently rejected any friendship to a certain person or only men or only women because at some time previously they had suffered an unpleasant experience in the hands of that particular person or a man or woman. In fact, it has been my experience that parrakeets in general are more friendly toward women and girls than men and boys, no doubt due to the fact that in their native land the women and girls usually have the responsibility of caring for the birds that the men have taken captive, stealing them from their nests. This is why most parrakeets that are brought into the bird trade have already been partially reared by hand in the land of their origin. The natives give the birds various sorts of cereals, special corn, and bananas. I am referring here only to the birds that come from South America. It is advisable to continue this menu temporarily if the birds are not yet eating independently. Even if the bird is eating independently, I would still advise you to continue this diet with, of course, the necessary supplements, which are described in the chapter dealing with feeding as well as under the descriptions of the individual species. Parrakeets and parrots drink very little. Nevertheless, we should daily offer them fresh water that has been boiled and then cooled off.

Recently imported birds often suffer from diarrhea due to the change in temperature and lack of proper nutrition. As previously mentioned, the use of antibiotics will soon have this condition under control. Housing, food, and temperature should fulfill the proper requirements. If your bird does not seem to improve very much, it would seem sensible to consult a veterinarian.

Keep in mind that parrakeets and parrots live in groups, so we should never keep one by itself, at least not for any extended period of time. If, however, we cannot or will not keep more than one, we should definitely spend some time with our pet every day. I firmly believe that the secret of success in keeping and caring for parrakeets lies hidden within the first few weeks. What is our attitude toward our bird? How do we take care of him? How sweet do we feel we can be to him? Etc., etc. The answers to all these questions will determine to a great extent the development of your bird and the relationship between the two of you. The lack of a partner (in the form of either another bird or its owner) will leave a mark on the behavior and development of the bird. This is also a good reason for supplying toys for your bird. Never give toys that are soft or made of rubber. A small cooked bone makes a nutritious toy with which the bird will enjoy playing, and it will give him some additional protein as well. Of course, this bone will have to be replaced or thrown out after a day, since it is an ideal breeding ground for bacteria.

It may happen that in a shipment of parrakeets there are some individuals that have a surprisingly dirty plumage. There are cans of spray available that will take care of this nicely, and for that matter a soft sponge with some clean water can do wonders as well. This type of clean-up has to take place in the morning so there is enough time for the feathers to dry before the bird goes to sleep. Feathers that are not completely dry cause a substantial loss of body heat, even in a heated aviary, which exposes the bird to catching a cold, intestinal upsets, and other such unpleasantries. Using the spray a few times will lead to a definite improvement, although a few broken feathers will do nothing to enhance your bird's appearance. Some fanciers choose to pull out these broken or damaged feathers so that new feathers can start to develop. I personally oppose this method strongly, because the growth of new feathers requires certain strengths from within the bird, and I hope I have already made it clear that our bird needs to reserve his strength for other matters at this point in time. Only when the bird has been totally acclimated and perhaps is being prepared for a bird show should we remove damaged or broken feathers. As all birds molt about once a year anyway, although there are certain parrakeets that may go a little longer than a year, we can generally state that a bird takes about twelve months to outfit himself with a new suit of feathers. During the molting time we must pay extra attention to ensure that our birds do not become subject to catching a cold, since their resistance to cold, damp, and drafts is considerably less during that period. Personally, I remove the dropped feathers (often three times a day) in an effort to prevent the birds from developing the bad habit of feather pecking either themselves or each other.

It is frequently asked whether tame parrakeets should be allow-

1. Follow the guidelines for selecting a good, healthy bird from a reliable merchant. 2. A few drops of antibiotics in cooled boiled water can do wonders for your new bird's health and appearance. 3. A cage for smaller birds. The cover can serve the dual purpose of quieting your bird when excited, a cue that it is time for sleep, and protecting your bird from drafts. 4. Compare this roomy cage to the cage pictured below (5), a cage that should be used only to transport your bird.

1   2

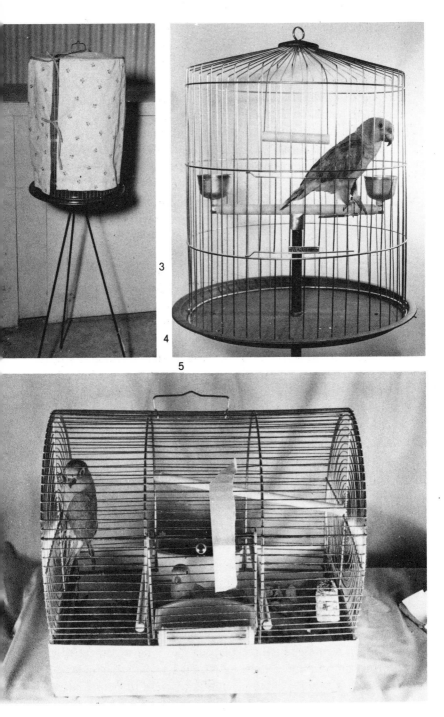

ed to fly freely within the home. Since I feel that birds should be given the roomiest housing possible, I see no reason why a tame parrakeet could not be given this freedom once or more often a week. Just be sure that it has no means of escape through doors or unscreened open windows. The bird will enjoy this freedom very much and usually will not even fly around all that much. Should your birds start to nibble at drapes or furniture, you should immediately put an end to their free flight. However, if we peacefully go about our own business and calmly forbid whatever we do not want our birds to do, damaging escapades are not likely to occur.

I would like to emphasize again the importance of always speaking to your birds in a friendly tone, never yelling at them to tell them off for some little slip they made from the straight and narrow path. Otherwise we may very well end up with real screamers that will stand your hair on end and disturb anyone else within earshot. Never frighten them or suddenly scare them, and never tease them. All these things will only help develop screeching personalities that you will have the pleasure of living with! Keep in mind, too, that a bird that is constantly kept inside may very well start to screech out of sheer boredom. Should you respond to screeches by running to your bird to see what all the ruckus is about, you will unconsciously be making a first class screamer of your pet. Parrakeets, and particularly tame ones, are much amused by every extra attention they can glean from their owners, and they will soon learn that raising their voices will set you running to them. If you allow yourself to be manipulated, you will become a valuable toy for their amusement. So what should we do? Simply ignore your bird if and when he starts to scream. If he continues to scream, put a cloth over his cage. This will serve as a punishment and generally works well to prevent further screaming.

What should you do when a bird escapes? In the first place, don't go chasing after him if he merely escapes inside the room, as this will only add to the confusion and cause him to crash into windows and knock over vases and other knick-knacks. If you do not have a net, throw a soft smooth towel over him as soon as he sits still for a moment. Make all your movements controlled and with the least amount of noise and unnecessary flailing of arms. If you do not succeed at catching him during the first attempt, give him some time to calm down before you try again. If his escape takes place during the evening, close the curtains, switch off all the lights, and use a flashlight. Parrots and parrakeets usually do not like flying about in the dark, although some Australian species love to do it in the wild as well as in large aviaries! In fact, a lamp that lights up just his cage may well encourage him to re-enter it by himself.

Should a bird escape outside, place a dish with food at the back door or on a window sill; in the event your bird is kept in an outside aviary, put it on top of the aviary. Try to keep everything as peaceful as possible: no children outside, no TV or radio on, etc. Wait until your bird comes to feed at the table you have set for it, then throw a net or tea towel over the bird. We could also use a garden hose to wet him down and keep him from flying away, but this can only be done if the temperature is relatively high. A bird trap could come in handy in this situation, placing it where you have observed your bird to be spending some time. It could also be placed in the immediate vicinity of the place where he usually spends the night, bearing in mind that these birds do not like to fly at night; in the morning while it is still dark, place your bird's favorite food in the trap. Should you have a trap with a double compartment, it would not hurt to place another bird of the same species in the second part as "bait." We can usually capture our bird quite easily like this, although without our "bait" it may take a good deal longer. Time, however, should not be of the essence where a valuable specimen is concerned.

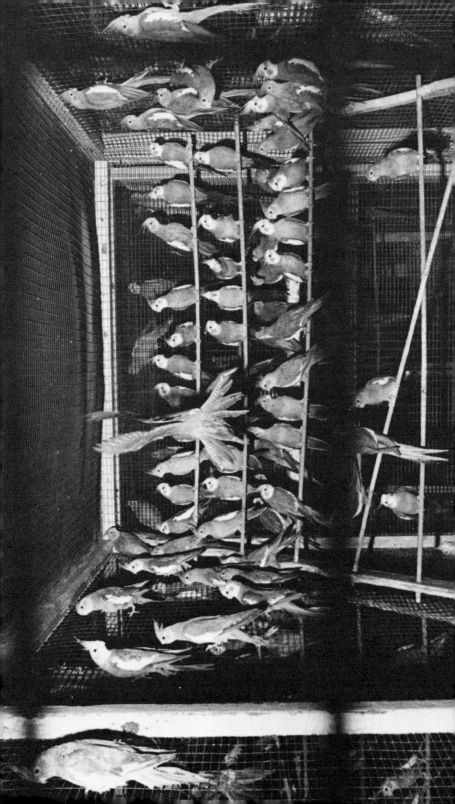

3. Cages and Aviaries

Young cockatiels are being temporarily
housed in this cage as they await buyers.

In order to take good care of parrakeets, we should be able to provide them with excellent housing, a cage or aviary in which the birds can comfortably fly around and which is easy to keep clean. Good housing facilitates the taming of our birds, helps to keep their feathers in good shape, and assures their state of health as a whole is better; hence they live longer.

Cages

One of the main comments we can make on cages is that there is yet to be constructed a cage that is too big for our feathered friends. Even the well known budgerigar likes spaciousness. This is why I am not in favor of keeping parrakeets in cages. However, circumstances may be such that we have no choice in the matter.

Cages should be constructed of metal because those made of wood and such soon fall victim to the insatiable gnawing habits of our birds. If you can solder, I suppose you could build your own cage, but I think that in the long run you would spend less money buying a cage in a pet shop. Almost every pet shop has a large selection of models, but the oblong shapes are my choice. For the larger species they should measure 55 x 50 cm and 85 cm high (22 x 20 x 34 inches), while the smaller species can be happy in a cage that is 40 x 35 cm and 60 cm (16 x 14 x 24 inches). The larger models are often equipped with a bottom that slides out, which simplifies cleaning and allows the bird to remain in the cage as well. Some have a double bottom, the top being made of wire bars like the rest of the cage. Personally I am not in favor of this variety, although it does mean that the birds do not step into their own feces. However, a compromise can be worked out here by covering part of the "grill" with a piece of grass sod, which of course will need to be replaced regularly. It is understandable that we should give an extra dish of grit to our birds if they are kept in a cage with a double bottom.

Even though you may be a "do-it-yourselfer," we still advise against a wooden cage. In spite of the fact that you may go to the trouble of covering the edges with metal strips, it will still just be a matter of time before the bird's gnawing damages the cage to the extent that it is no longer attractive and may end up in the garage, complete with bird . . . hardly ideal air- and light-wise!

The Alexandrine ringneck parrakeet, *Psittacula eupatria nipalensis,* is the largest member of its genus. Compared to the Indian ringneck, the Alexandrine parrakeet (as it is also called) seems topheavy: the large head and huge bill seem out of proportion. There is a patch of deep red on the wings. Females have the pink and black on the neck. This bird is a popular favorite and a fair breeder. Because of its greater rarity, the Alexandrine is more expensive than the Indian ringneck.

PERCHES

Perches are made of a hardwood such as beech and should not be too thin; 22 mm thick (7/8 inch) is ideal. Nor should they be too smooth; in fact, we should roughen them with sandpaper each time we clean the cage. Our birds have to get their rest on the perches, and they can't do this when the perches are too thin or too smooth. Their toes must comfortably clutch the perch in such a manner that the feet almost encircle the thickness of the perch, but not completely. The perches should be round but slightly flattened on the top to help prevent excessive growth of the nails. We advise using only hardwood perches because anything else would never last very long against the bird's gnawing. Softwood also has the disadvantage of being a good hiding place for insects, bacteria, and other undesirable inhabitants of our bird's cage. Perches that are too thin are also bad in that the toes will be hanging to the point where they are no longer protected by the feathers on the stomach when the bird is in a resting position. During the winter months this is very important, because if the feet are not adequately kept warm by these feathers the bird will suffer from frozen toes. A good sitting or sleeping perch will allow the bird to rest comfortably and completely, and the stomach feathers will properly protect the feet.

To satisfy their gnawing desires and distract them from taking out these desires on the perches, we should give the birds twigs with which they can play and chew to their hearts' content. Twigs from apple, pear, plum, and cherry trees are ideal. These twigs should be dried first (two weeks are sufficient). In the aviary we can provide our birds with perches of various thicknesses, both stationary and swinging types, while the shrubbery we plant in the aviary will provide quite a few resting places as well. Stationary perches should be placed in the inside area, thereby more or less forcing our birds to spend the night in the sheltered part. When your birds have developed the habit of sleeping in the night shelter, you will not be greeted with unpleasant surprises during the winter months. We can reinforce this habit even more by placing the stationary perches in high locations, particularly in the night shelter, because birds will instinctively go to the highest perches to sleep. Providing extra branches for climbing in the corners of the aviary is highly recommended, because live shrubs and small trees are generally not guaranteed a very long life in an aviary with gnawing birds.

FOOD AND WATER DISHES

Dishes should be placed where no bird droppings can fall into them, such as would be the case if they were placed underneath any perches. They should also be easily accessible to the bird keeper, since both food and water dishes should be cleaned daily. Naturally the seed dishes should be dried thoroughly before re-filling them with seed. I recommend the use of automatic feeding containers for seed and flat earthenware saucers for water. There should always be a cuttle available for our birds, as this provides some necessary minerals and is also excellent in helping to keep the beak in good shape.

BATHING FACILITIES

Not all parrakeets like to take a bath, and certainly not when they are kept in cages. There are little metal "bathhouses" that can be affixed to the opening of the cage, but many species will never use them. They far prefer to frolic outside on a flat earthenware saucer, under a dripping faucet, or under a softly squirting garden hose. With tame birds this can easily be realized, but untamed birds will first have to become accustomed to their cage, their surroundings, and their keeper before we can offer them a bath. In any event, be sure your birds are completely dry before they retire for the night. I can see no objection to placing bird and cage outside on a warm day and letting the garden hose softly drizzle on one side of it, to the greatest amusement of our bird. Obviously, we have removed the seed dish and the sand-covered bottom of the cage so we will be able to dry everything off as efficiently as possible when we take bird and cage back inside.

LOCATION OF THE CAGE

The location of the parrakeet cage plays a significant role in the successful keeping of these birds. Parrakeets (and parrots for that matter) do not like to be alone; they like to belong to, and have the

1. Derbyan parrakeets, *Psittacula derbiana,* from the remote areas of southeast Tibet and southwest China. 2. and 3. Plum-headed parrakeet, *P.c. cyanocephala,* a beautiful bird that is very tolerant towards other parrakeets, even towards little finches. 4. Malabar parrakeets, *P. columboides,* a rare native from southwestern India. 5. Rose-ringed parrakeet, *P. krameri manillensis.*

2

3

4

5

companionship of, the human family. They like to be placed in an area where they can observe all that goes on in the home. We should place the cage in a sunny location, although not directly in the sunlight, of course, since they must have the opportunity to move to a shady spot if they want. In other words, part sun and part shade would be ideal. However, since the sun follows a set course, it may happen that at a certain time of the day the cage is completely within the rays of the sun. This is not good. Do not suppose that since parrakeets come from the tropics they will be used to sitting in and liking the sun. Although they may come from the warm regions, the time they spend in direct sunlight is very limited, since they spend the largest part of their day in the shelter of the lush foliage of jungle trees. In choosing a location it is also very important that there is absolutely no draft. Therefore, avoid a location that is between doors and windows or in a corridor or hallway that has a door going outside. If the temperature generally remains the same both day and night, there is no need to cover the cage at night.

Aviaries

If we have the intention of breeding our birds, we will need to have aviaries available to them. There are many models to choose from, but I think the most success is achieved by constructing a number of small aviaries (at least 2 x 1½ x 2 meters or 6 x 4½ x 6 ft.) since most parrakeets will not tolerate each other during the breeding season. The aviary must consist of a shelter and a flight. If we make our aviaries of wood, we will need to use metal strips and wire mesh to protect it from gnawing little beaks.

LOCATION

The aviary should be built in a location that is as dry as possible and is the least affected by winds. The front of the aviary should face south. Plant hardy shrubs and small trees to provide plenty of shade.

1

2

1. Outdoor aviary for small parrakeets, canaries or finches or for use as a baby-pen. 2. Rear view of batteries of all-metal breeding cages. 3. Indoor cages for parrots and parrakeets before the birds go into quarantine.

3

A male Javan parakeet, *Psittacula a. alexandri;* this subspecies is from Java and Bali and has been introduced to the southern parts of Borneo. In this subspecies, the female also has a red bill.

The slaty-headed parrakeet, *P.h. himalayana,* resembles the female plum-headed parrakeet except that it is larger. This species is from the Himalayas and is rare in captivity.

1. This closeup of a self-watering set-up shows the continuous fresh water supply dripping from a small pipe. 2. Shade is essential for your birds' comfort and general well-being. 3. The ideal aviary; it offers ample room for exercise for even the largest members of the parrot family. 4. An outdoor aviary for small parrakeets and such.

2

3

4

The blue rose-ringed parrakeet, *Psittacula krameri manillensis*, (opposite) inherits its color as an autosomal recessive. The lutino (above) inherits as a sex-linked recessive. This mutation has been known for more than 200 years!

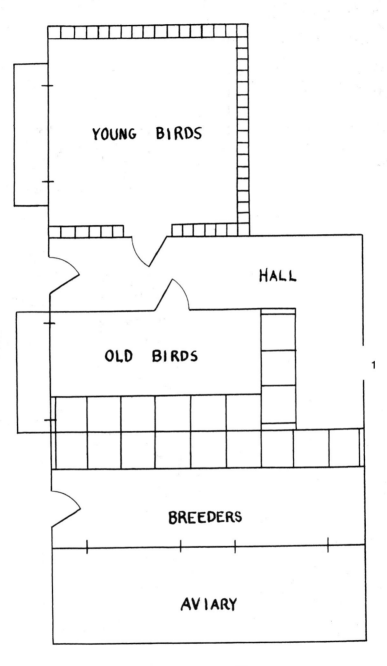

FLOOR PLAN

2

3

1. A floor plan for an out-door aviary. 2. A beautiful garden birdroom for delicate parrakeets. 3. A practical and inexpensive aviary consisting of large flights and closed-in shelter.

The nanday conure, *Nandayus nenday,* pictured here with the author's hand, deserves honorable mention for its cooperation and patience in posing for several of the photographs for this book. (Dr. Vriends also deserves an honorable mention, as he did not lose his patience when the nanday's ran out and it decided to bite Dr. Vriends' finger.)

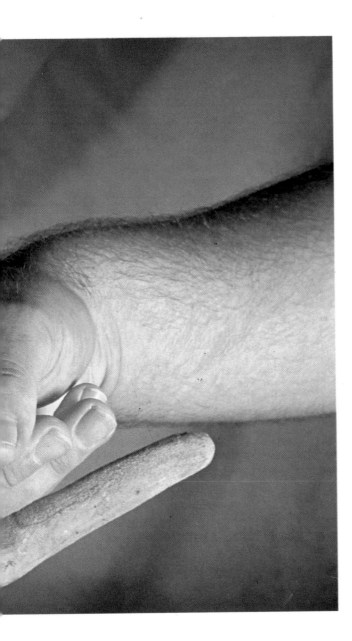

FLOOR

Although a natural earthen floor has a lot of advantages, I think that a cement or concrete floor is the better choice when we wish to breed parrakeets. On this floor, we can place large pots containing plants or we can arrange to pour the concrete in such a way as to reserve a number of spots for planting shrubs. A cement floor can be hosed off daily, ridding it of any droppings and other messes the birds have made, or the floor could be sprinkled with sand or grit that should be replaced every two weeks. Part of the floor could be planted with sod; many birds very much enjoy frolicking on grass moist with dew or under the gentle spray of a garden hose. If you find it impossible to keep the sod alive, place it in low wooden boxes so that they can be removed whenever you wish to check or replace them without upsetting the birds.

DOORS

It does not make much difference where you place your doors, as long as you remember to build two of them to form a little "foyer" in an effort to prevent your birds from escaping while you come into or leave the aviary. It is advisable to divide the flight from the shelter with a door as well; in this manner we can force our birds to amuse themselves in the protected night shelter during particularly cold and nasty weather by simply closing the door.

PERCHES IN THE AVIARY

Perches should be made of hardwood like those used in cages. Provide your birds with twigs and small branches from fruit trees so they can aim their gnawing attacks on these rather than to the perches, which are not all that inexpensive. Another advantage of providing twigs for gnawing is that they won't start the bad habit of pecking at each other's feathers. Affix the perches at both ends of the flight so they do not interfere with the length of the flight available to the birds. Perches should not be installed too close to the wire, however, both because of cats, which can pose a definite danger, and because the birds' tail feathers would eventually become frayed when they are constantly rubbed against the wire. If we can place an old tree trunk in the center of the aviary or build the aviary around one, we should by all means do this.

BATHING FACILITIES IN THE AVIARY

Every aviary should be equipped with flat earthenware saucers allowing the birds to take a bath. On colder days, of course, we should remove these dishes. Make sure that your birds are dry before they go to sleep; that is, they should not have the opportunity to bathe after four or five p.m. We could also put a garden sprinkler to good use, as many birds prefer this to a bath. Ponds with rocks and running water are obviously idyllic, but unfortunately not something that everyone can afford. Perches, of course, should not be situated above any of these bathing or drinking facilities. The water in the saucers should be changed daily.

WATER AND SEED DISHES IN THE AVIARY

Directions that are given in the chapter dealing with feeding obviously pertain to both the fancier who keeps one bird in a cage and the fancier who keeps several aviaries. However, one must realize that a bird that lives in an aviary has a great deal more room for flying and hence gets a lot more exercise, so that fat-containing seeds such as hemp, sunflower seeds, linseed, maw, rape and peanuts can be given in greater quantities. We should use indestructible seed feeders that are easily cleaned and made so the parrakeets cannot soil their contents in any way and cannot sit or walk on seeds. Wooden feeders, of course, would soon be reduced to splinters. There are several feeders on the market. Your pet shop is sure to be able to advise you on them. Saucers made of glass, ceramics, and such are suitable as well and are most often used both for seed and for water.

The most practical feeders, however, are the box-like hoppers with glass fronts called self-feeders. These hoppers usually hold quantities of seeds sufficient for a number of days. They are often divided into a few narrow compartments in which each kind of seed is given separately, enabling the birds to make their own mixture to suit their needs. Around the bottom of these feeders extends a detachable tray that is designed to catch seeds thrown aside by the parrakeets.

The Alexandrine ringneck parrakeet, *Psittacula eupatria nipalensis,*
above and opposite, appears to be a gross caricature of the ringneck,
but in reality the bird is not out of proportion and holds an attitude of
majestic nature which the ringneck does not possess.

4. Feeding Parrakeets

A pair of turquoise parrots (also called turquoisine grass parrakeets). These birds have one of the strongest pet potentials for everybody. They are easily trained while young, reasonable in price and attractive in appearance.

1   2

56

1. The Sierra parrakeet, *Bolborhynchus aymara*, is distributed along the eastern slopes of the Andes. 2. The Cape parrot, *Poicephalus robustus*, is from southern and central Africa. 3. The plum-headed parrakeet, *Psittacula cyanocephala*, is found in Sri Lanka (Ceylon) and most of the Indian subcontinent.

It is our intention to include in detail the feeding requirements in the descriptions of the individual species. Without a good menu, our birds cannot remain happy and healthy. When we purchase new birds we should find out exactly how the previous owner fed them so we can continue this diet temporarily. Only gradually should we accustom our new birds to any changes in the diet; any sudden changes may cause intestinal upsets within our birds, and this of course should be avoided.

Most fanciers serve seeds in a pre-mixed form; many excellent mixes are available on the market, and we can also mix our own formula. As probably almost everyone knows, parrakeets are basically seed-eaters. An excellent mixture would be of sunflower seeds, oats, millet, white seed and hemp, all in equal amounts. If so desired, we can add linseed, which is a seed that has a high fat level (35.5%) and is rich in proteins (25.5%) and therefore an ideal supplement during cold weather. I would like to make a few remarks about hemp. Specifically, I believe we should only mix a small amount of hemp, as indicated by a mixture I give to most of my parrakeets: 45% La Plata millet, 5% white panicum millet, 25% Morocco white seed, 15%-18% sunflower seeds, and only 3-5% hemp seed. During the breeding period or, more accurately, when the fledglings are in the nest, we can increase this to 8% hemp.

Never buy old seed, since this has lost much of its value. To check on whether or not we have received fresh seed from our local dealer, we can conduct the following test: sprinkle some seed on a saucer containing a thin layer of lukewarm water; replace the water twice a day, and place the saucer in a light, airy location; if the seed germinates in three to four days, it is fresh. If this process takes considerably longer, we should switch our seed source.

Keep a close eye on the seed feeder and clean it whenever necessary so that mold, bacteria, and insects such as earwigs and roaches do not have a chance to do their destructive work. It speaks for itself that we should place the seed in a dry spot, preferably in the center, so that all our birds have easy access to it.

Parrakeets are not totally satisfied with just seed, even if we very wisely vary the mixture once in a while by adding weed seeds, grass seed, and niger. If we want our birds to be in excellent physical condition, we should regularly give them universal food, soft food (nestling food), fruit (such as apples, pears, cherries, berries, pieces of banana, oranges, soaked raisins and currants, and peanuts), live foods (anteggs, mealworms, whiteworms, beetles, small spiders, grasshoppers, etc.), and greens (Brussel sprouts, cauliflower, young dandelion leaves, lettuce, endive, spinach, red cabbage, etc.). Giving them grated carrots and chickweed can only do them good. If you want to give your birds a real treat, a slice of bread spread with peanut butter and soaked in milk or water will utterly delight them. They also like to feed this to their young. Giving them an extra portion of unroasted peanuts during the breeding season is practically a must; the rich oils are very nutritious for the birds.

During the breeding period our birds should also have available seeding grasses and sprouted seeds, as well as grit and cuttlebone. The latter two, together with charcoal of course, should be available year-round. Cuttlebone that is found on the beach contains too much salt to be offered directly to the birds. It should be soaked in water for a few days, changing the water three to four times a day. We can then hang it inside the aviary on special holders or with a piece of wire through it. Naturally, cuttlebone that is bought in the store is ready for immediate consumption by your birds and comes complete with a holder. Grit is a necessary element in the digestive system of our birds, since their food is virtually 'ground' inside the stomach. It is also necessary for the forming of bone. Cuttlebone serves to supplement any shortages in calcium and is good for forming the eggshells in the female. As you can see, calcium is imperative for the good growth of both young birds (forming a sturdy skeleton) and older birds (in the breeding period). Grit contains calcium, charcoal, iron, magnesium, and iodine. Cuttlebone contains important salts in addition to those elements that make up grit.

Universal food and soft food (also called nestling food) should be given on flat earthenware saucers. Never offer more than the birds can consume in one day, because these foods will spoil very easily. Neither should these dishes be placed in direct sunlight; a better place would be in the night shelter or, if your aviary consists of three parts (night shelter, covered and uncovered flights), in the covered flight where it is protected from both sun and rain.

With regard to giving live food, here are a couple of warnings.

1. The White-eared conure, *Pyrrhura leucotis,* is from the northern parts of Venezuela and eastern Brazil. It was introduced to Rio de Janeiro Botanic Gardens! 2. The blossom-headed parrakeet, *Psittacula roseata,* likes a nestbox of 10 x 12 inches. 3. The crimson-bellied conure, *Pyrrhura rhodogaster,* is known for its constant chatter. 4. The red-bellied conure, *P. frontalis,* from southeastern Brazil, is one of the most typical species of the genus.

4

1

2

3

4

1. Sprouted seed should be available for your birds during breeding season. 2. All types of equipment for your bird can be purchased in most pet shops. 3. A variety of water dishes and automatic feed dispensers. 4. A manufactured mineral block used for a beak trimmer. 5. A good supply of seeds is available at your pet shop.

5

1. The cactus conure, *Aratinga c. cactorum,* from Brazil, is rare in the U.S., probably because of its dull coloration. 2. The peach-fronted conure, *A. aurea,* comes from Brazil and northwestern Argentina. It has a very bright orange forehead. 3. The bee-bee or tovi parrakeet, *Brotogeris jugularis,* is very well known. It becomes reasonably tame and occasionally is a good talker. 4. The Moustached parrakeet, *Psittacula alexandri fasciata,* is very attractive. The bill of the male is red, the hen's is black. 5. The monk parrakeet, *Myiopsitta monachus.*

Do not give too much, particularly if the live food consists of mealworms. Large parrakeet varieties can be given 8-10 mealworms per day per bird, and 2-3 worms will suffice for smaller species. Small mealworms can be fed to young birds, but they should first be boiled; place them in an old nylon stocking and submerge in boiling water for three minutes. Live mealworms cannot do much damage to the wall of the crop in older birds, but in the case of young birds they could cause very unpleasant problems, since the worms can eat their way through the wall of the young bird's crop.

To achieve the best possible health of our birds, particularly during the period in which they breed, regularly give them stale bread soaked in milk or water with about 5-8 drops of vitamins added. Offering ordinary cod liver oil (3-4 drops per kilo, 2.2 pounds) mixed in with the seed produces satisfactory results as well.

When we offer our birds—in addition to all of the above—a good, roomy aviary and sufficient breeding boxes, I am convinced that they will have long and healthy lives and will successfully breed on a regular basis.

5. Breeding Parrakeets

2

1. The canary-winged conure, *Brotogeris versicolorus versicolorus,* occurs in the interior of Brazil in flocks of from eight or ten to up to more than fifty birds; it is very noisy. 2. The white-eyed conure, *Aratinga leucophthalmus,* is fairly common; it usually lives in pairs or family parties. 3. The Derbyan parrakeet, *Psittacula derbiana,* also lives in family parties or small flocks in forested areas.

3

Under the individual descriptions of the various species, I will go into detail about such things as the particular breeding boxes required, what type of nest inspections should be made, how the young should be reared, etc., but in this chapter I would like to make some general remarks and also delve into the matter of using incubators. The breeding of parrakeets has developed considerably during the last few years, and it is a well known fact that the current intensive breeding has saved several species from extinction. In fact, in some cases there are more specimens in captivity of a certain species than there are living in the wild!

We could conclude from the above that the breeding of parrakeets is a relatively simple matter. However, this does not imply we will have the same success with all species. If we keep within the guidelines that will be given later, we can be assured that the majority of our pets will provide us with offspring. Although the Australian varieties seem to be the most popular, they often give the most problems when it comes to breeding. Should we be in possession of a good pair, then even the Australian parrakeets will come through the breeding process successfully. After all, most fanciers are not loath to experiment once or twice. It is important that you keep a watchful eye on your birds so you will soon know exactly what they want from you—I am thinking here of food and breeding boxes.

It is also very important that we house each pair separately. As already stated, this will produce the best breeding results. Never place two pairs together in one aviary (unless stated to the contrary in the individual descriptions of the species). We strongly advise against this, as it will only lead to fighting between the males, unfertilized eggs, and other such unpleasant results. If we have an aviary that is divided into several *ROOMY* compartments, we never place two couples of the same species or closely related species in neighboring compartments, but instead place unrelated species in the compartments that fall between. Even then we will have to keep in mind which birds can be crossed with a certain species, because "closely related" could include several species that ornithologically do not belong to the same genus but in captivity become very interested in each other, so that crossing is altogether possible. The red-winged parrot, belonging to the genus *Aprosmictus (A. erythropterus)*, can be crossed with the regent parrot *(Polytelis anthopeplus)*, which belongs to an entirely different genus. Keeping an eye out is obviously necessary.

I can well imagine that many fanciers may feel somewhat at a loss after reading the above; after all, the available space that most fanciers have to work with is usually somewhat limited and could make the suggestions difficult to realize. For this reason we would add that the above can be taken with a grain of salt. The following general rule should suffice: never place birds of the same species together or next to each other in an aviary, and place birds of the same genus as far apart as possible. This notation should allow the necessary freedom; we should do what is possible, what can be realized.

I suppose I need not draw your attention to the fact that we should keep everything as peaceful as possible, even outside the aviary, during the breeding period. If we keep dogs or cats (are there bird breeders who really keep cats?), then these should not be allowed in the garden where our aviary is situated, although I usually have one or more dogs that roam freely in my garden; it is surprising how well and how quickly birds become accustomed to dogs. We should conduct ourselves as quietly and calmly as possible, particularly when we are inspecting the aviary, because it does not take much to upset a bird enough for it to desert its nest. It is therefore important that we keep to a fixed schedule for feeding and providing drinking and bathing water for our birds. They will become used to you in no time at all, especially if you make a habit of softly singing or whistling whenever you need to be near or go into the aviary; this has a surprisingly calming effect on the birds. Only when we offer our birds a peaceful existence can we count on excellent breeding results.

BREEDING FACILITIES

Parrots and parrakeets generally don't use nesting materials in building their nests. The monk parrakeet and lovebirds build a sophisticated nest, but they are the exception to the rule, and ornithologists are still wondering about this. We will, therefore, have to give our pets a hand and can do this by providing them with artificial breeding facilities. In the wild several species will build a small 'egg hollow' or nest cavity (this term is really a euphemism

1. The Cuban conure, *Aratinga euops,* is also called the red-speckled or Euops conure. There are red flecks on the sides of the head and at the bend of the wing, with a solid red on the underwing coverts. 2. and 3. The red-fronted conure, *Aratinga wagleri,* or Wagler's conure, is from Colombia and the northern coastal region of western Venezuela. According to Forshaw, it is a noisy parrot that undertakes regular daily flights between its roosting sites and feeding grounds.

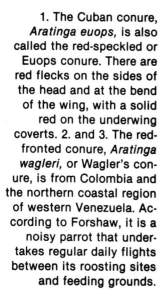

3

2

3

4

1. Plum-headed parrakeet, *Psittacula cyanocephala.* 2. Mexican, or turquoise-rumped parrotlet. Attractive green is highlighted by a bright turquoise blue on the rump, greater wing coverts and under the wing. Females lack the blue. 3. The sierra parrakeet, *Bolborhynchus aymara,* is most graceful in a large outdoor aviary. A true pair is worth watching during the mating period; they seem to embrace one another with their wings and sit cheek to cheek. 4. Finsch's conure is an attractive red and green conure with red on the head almost restricted to the forehead.

75

1

2

1. and 3. The golden conure, *Aratinga guarauba,* is one of the rarest, most expensive and most striking of all conures. The bird is an overall brilliant golden yellow, with rich green flight feathers. This parrakeet is uncommon in captivity; it lives in tropical rain-forests in pairs of small groups and is becoming increasingly rare in the wild. In captivity, only the hen incubates the two to three white eggs, but the male roosts with her in the nestbox during the night. 2. The canary-winged conure, *Brotogeris versicolorus versicolorus,* is a very charming but noisy bird that has a direct and swift flight.

3

1   2

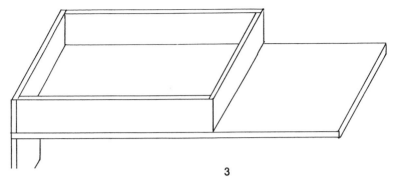

3

78

1. White millet spray is a treat for every bird. 2. All kinds of minerals are necessary, especially during the breeding season. 3. A diagram of a parrot feeding box. 4. White worms are taken by some birds, so it is worthwhile to supply them. 5. Keep your bird's water dish clean and filled with water.

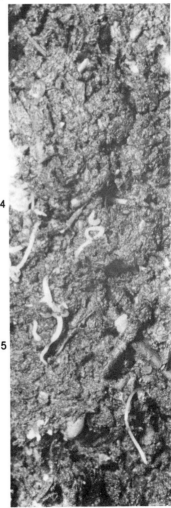

4

5

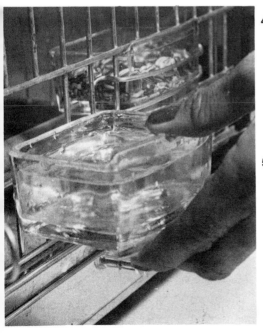

Scarlet-chested parrot, *Neophema splendida.* This beautiful species breeds very well in captivity.

in this case) made of little twigs and splinters on which to deposit their eggs; in captivity we would try to imitate this arrangement in a nesting box. Each couple should be provided with at least two different types of nesting boxes so they can select the one they prefer and not be forced to be content with just one type of nesting box. I find that the most success is achieved by providing four boxes (two different types), of which I hang two in the uncovered flight and two in the night shelter, both types on the same wall. If after a week and a half the birds still show no interest in breeding (which can be determined by the birds' not bothering to inspect the nesting boxes), I move the boxes to the opposite wall. You may wonder why I do not hang one box on each wall. The answer to this is simple: since it is not possible to determine ahead of time which nesting box the birds prefer, we hang the boxes first on one wall; when this does not inspire breeding, we move them to the opposite wall. Of course, be sure to use a location where inspections can be made without causing too much of an upheaval. When we know after a few breeding seasons which type and location the birds prefer, we can stick to just the favored type, but first we must determine which one leads to the best results.

It may happen, and is in fact not at all uncommon, that one of our pairs simply refuses to breed, even though they are given the right food and the correct type of breeding boxes. We may be dealing with "travelling birds". . .birds that move from one owner to the next because they will not breed. In this case, we will either have to accept this fact or we might try to return one or both of them to the previous owner, explaining to him the vital shortcomings of the birds. We previously stressed the importance of arranging for an exchange or return possibility with the seller when buying birds. If the birds are still young, it would be wise to exchange one of them, preferably the male, for a new mate for the female. Changing partners like that sometimes brings about the desired results immediately. It is common, particularly with some of the sturdier species, to obtain excellent results after years of no breeding once the partners have been changed. Incest or inbreeding is something we want to avoid unless we are trying to adhere to or establish certain mutations, such as took place with the white collared rose-ringed parrakeets of Dr. L.A. Swaenepoel from Lembeek, Belgium.

Breeding boxes are best made out of natural tree trunks that are hollowed out and provided with a round hole. Instead of nailing down the lid, it is more practical to affix one or more hinges so that we can easily take a peek into the nest and later clean it more conveniently. There are nesting boxes made of birch, plywood, and other woods available on the market, complete with a little entrance hole and the hollowed-out nest cavity where the eggs will come to lie. These boxes are too small for the majority of parrakeet species but will suffice for birds belonging to the genus *Neophema*, that is, the turquoise parrot, the elegant parrot, Bourke's parrot, scarlet-chested parrot, and such. The rosella species, on the other hand, require a nesting box that is about 45 cm long (18 inches) and has a diameter of about 25 cm (10 inches) or a few centimeters less; it should not be larger. I can imagine that it is not a simple matter to hollow out a breeding box of these dimensions, but you can saw the trunk in half lengthwise so hollowing it out is then a good deal easier. The two halves should be glued back together with care, using plaster, thin cement, or a good wood glue so that we will not end up with cracks after everything has dried out, because gusty winds could cause drafts through these openings that would mean dangerous consequences for both the breeding birds and the offspring.

The round entrance hole should be situated about 8-10 cm (3¼-4 inches) under the lid and have a diameter of 8 cm (3¼ inches) at most. About 4-5 cm. (1¾-2 inches) under the lid is the appropriate place for a few ventilation holes. Quite often the mother bird sits in the entrance hole for a while to get a breath of fresh air, with the unfortunate result that her body pretty well blocks the entire opening to the nest. The flow of oxygen into the nest is consequently partially or completely restricted and can be rather unpleasant for the little fledglings. When there are two or three more babies in the nest it takes little or no time to use up the available fresh air. This is why it is imperative that we drill the ventilation holes, which should be about 1 cm (2/5 inch) in diameter, thus eliminating all suffocation possibilities.

Besides transforming tree trunks into nesting boxes, we can also use smooth planks of wood, following the same sizes as the tree trunk nests. One of the advantages of making our boxes from cut wood rather than tree trunks is that they are easier to make and are

Above and opposite: The sun conure, *Aratinga solstitialis*, is most likely conspecific with the jandaya conure and golden-capped conure, *A. jandaya* and *A. auricapilla*.

1

1. A cage must be big enough to comfortably accommodate the bird. 2. A bird bath and a cuttlefish bone in holder. 3. Moscow bird market. 4. Youngsters interested in keeping birds must be properly educated as to the correct care of the equipment as well.

2

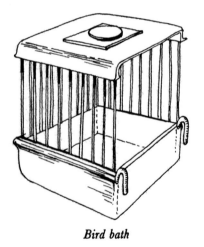

Bird bath

Cuttlefish bone in holder

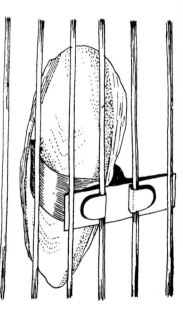

3   4

1. The red-bellied conure, also called maroon-bellied conure, *Pyrrhura frontalis,* is from south-eastern Brazil, Uruguay, Paraguay and northern Argentina. 2. The Aymara parrakeet, *Amoropsittaca aymara,* is also called the Sierra or grey-headed parrakeet.

1

2

3. The grey-cheeked parrakeet, *Brotogeris pyrrhopterus,* has its habitat in the arid tropical zones of Peru and Ecuador. 4. The lineolated parrakeet, *B.l. liniola,* occurs from Mexico to Panama. Its tail is one of its most expressive features; whenever the bird shows emotions, the tail fans outward in an unusual gesture.

3

4

lighter in weight, which cuts out the possibility that sooner or later they may fall down.

For large species such as the Barraband parrakeet, king parrakeet, and the like we should use tree trunks that are at least 1.50 meters (4½ feet) high. It is inadvisable to use trunks that are higher than 2 meters (6 feet). Under the entrance hole, measuring 8 cm (3¼ inches) in diameter, affix a few hooks to the inside of the box and attach to these a narrow strip of wire that will serve as a ladder to help the birds in climbing out of the box. Check the wire for sharp points that might injure the bird. These nesting boxes are placed on the ground and slightly tilted for obvious reasons (climbing). This same type of nesting box can be made of regular cut wood too, of course. The width (in this case from corner to corner) should be no less than 20 cm. (8 inches) and no more than 25 cm (10 inches). Although the birds use practically no nesting materials, quite a few species use a little grass, wool, strips of paper, bark, horse hair, feathers, jute, moss and wood mold to fill up the nest cavity. The latter two should be offered in a moist condition, and we can place these in the nest hollow ourselves if the birds do not do it themselves.

I would like to make a point regarding the age of the birds that we wish to breed. Birds that belong to the smaller species should be at least eight months old before we attempt to breed them. Larger varieties should be ten to twelve months old. After four to five years most parrakeets are no longer suitable for breeding, but there are many exceptions to this rule. I know birds that after ten years still breed and rear very good clutches and can compare very well with their younger counterparts.

INCUBATORS

I feel it is perfectly acceptable to use an incubator or any other type of electric "surrogate mother," particularly in the case of rare and expensive species. It is a costly loss to the aviculturist when a brood is lost due to the death of the female. In addition to the financial side, which· is certainly a relevant issue to the professional breeder, man can use artificial means such as incubators in an effort to prevent extinction of rare species, which must, no doubt, be considered as the most important issue of all: basically man restoring what man has upset. These electric machines have saved many a species from extinction. I am thinking in particular of a few very valuable Australian parrakeet species that would most definitely have become extinct had it not been for these mechanical mothers.

Unfortunately, it happens far too often that the female does not return to the nest to hatch the eggs she has just laid. This lack of desire to hatch her eggs can be caused by several factors. Feeding and housing seem to have an important influence on this desire. If these two requirements are up to par, we will seldom experience the female's unwillingness to hatch her eggs. However, it happens in the best of aviaries with the best of care. In most cases, the female will start sitting on the eggs after the third egg has been laid. If we see that the female has not started to sit on them after the third (and sometimes fourth) egg, we must take swift action if the eggs are to be saved. When the clutch is complete, but the female is no longer interested in them, carefully remove the eggs and put them in a cool place. There they will remain unspoiled for ten to twelve days, perhaps longer. It is not normally necessary to keep the eggs of any length of time, but I imagine that a breeder might want to know how long eggs may be kept.

We could place the eggs under another brooding female, but the clutch might become too big and we could end up losing both broods. An incubator, then, is the only solution. Personally, I place the eggs of a female who will not hatch them in my incubator when another female (possibly of same species) begins to hatch a clutch of her own. After six days we place all the eggs into the machine, including the clutch that belongs to the prospective foster parents; all unfertilized eggs are destroyed and replaced with good eggs from the machine (I am speaking of the eggs of the female that is willing to sit). Obviously, we do not just place the eggs in her nest, but wait for an opportune moment, such as when she leaves the nest for a few minutes to stretch her wings or perhaps when she is being fed nearby by the male. It is helpful to know that often species that are totally unrelated but of roughly the same size will adopt one or two foster children; however, it is wiser if we choose the same species to be foster parents. Red-rumped parrakeets, incidentally, are excellent foster parents. More than once bird breeders have discovered that a nest of young

The Mexican conure, or green conure, *A.h. holochlora,* is an unpretentious bird; some individuals have red flecks on the chest. It inhabits eastern and southern Mexico.

Petz's conure, (also known as orange-fronted conure and halfmoon conure), *Aratinga canicularis eburnirostrum,* is from western Mexico and is one of the most popular birds in the U.S. It is almost always sold as a "dwarf parrot" and is quite reasonable in cost.

1. In order to get success in breeding, humidity is very important. 2. The majority of the birds like some nesting material in the box, but not too much, otherwise they will toss the excess out. 3. In order to save room in the aviary, boxes can be hung outside. 4. Give your birds a choice between a nest box (left) and a natural tree trunk for nesting (right).

3

4

The golden-capped conure, *A. auricapilla,* is from eastern Brazil from Bahia south to the Rio Grande do Sul. This bird is closely related to the jandaya conure, from northeastern Brazil.

The peach-fronted conure, *Aratinga aurea,* is very common in the wild (savannah woodland). It is an excellent and affectionate pet if tamed young.

birds that were hatched by parrakeets actually consisted of four or more different species! Another good foster parent for smaller species, as well as red-rumped parrakeets and paradise parrakeets, is Bourke's parrot, while rosella species are good foster parents for all sorts of rosella varieties. Even lovebirds, budgerigars, and cockatiels can serve as foster parents for the smaller parrakeet varieties. Lovebirds make excellent foster parents for rosellas, Bourke's, elegants, turquoise, and similar parrots, while budgies are only fairly good for turquoise parrots. Quite a few breeders have separate pairs that are used exclusively as foster parents and which have never raised a clutch of their own. My experience here is that the best results are obtained with pairs that have never hatched and reared their own clutch or perhaps have only hatched their eggs. This is particularly the case with cockatiels. Regardless, be prepared to take a risk, as the chances of success or failure are sometimes only 50-50.

After checking out the eligible foster parents, we come to the actual use of the machine. Personally, I have the most success with a smaller model electric incubator that is equipped with a horizontal egg tray made of fine wire. A piece of jute covers the wire so that the young chicks will not end up with their feet sticking through the wire, which could result in broken legs or feet. The breeding apparatus is heated with warm air that blows onto the eggs and goes out through the ventilation opening(s) located at the bottom or one of the sides of the machine. The temperature immediately above the eggs is approximately $39^0 C.$; *I have the best results with a constant temperature of 39.5° C. (105° F.).* A thermostat regulates the temperature. If the unit does not already come with a thermometer we should purchase one to check if the unit is working at the proper temperature. The thermometer should be placed just above the eggs against one of the sides so that the little mercury bulb is at the same level as the eggs. An incubator unit has double walls for insulation purposes to provide an even heat. I recommend the use of an ether capsule thermostat, since it is the most sensitive, hence the most accurate; the bimetallic thermostat is not as sensitive, although quite popular due to its sturdiness.

I am sure that most of us have heard at one time or another that birds turn their eggs several times per day, for obvious reasons.

Since we do not have a bird in the incubator to do this for us, we will have to do it ourselves. Don't worry that the opening of the door will cool off the eggs too much; in fact, this breath of fresh air is even good for the proper growth of the egg. We should turn the eggs twice a day, in the morning around eight o'clock (so before you leave for work), and at night around nine o'clock. At these times also make sure that there is enough water in the water container at the bottom of the unit. This is imperative for the successful hatching of the eggs; without the proper humidity, the eggs will dry up inside. Many people use a hygrometer, which is a device to measure the moisture in the air; I consider this precaution a little far-fetched and certainly not necessary. Exercise caution when turning the eggs. . .perhaps a plastic spoon may be useful in this delicate operation.

Once the eggs begin to show peck-marks or are ready to hatch, we can place them under a brooding hen; her own clutch should be removed and is generally regarded as lost, but we can, of course, place them in the incubator too, so that we have made, so to speak, a complete circle. If we have more mating pairs, we can distribute the hen's eggs among them, assuming that these pairs have all started to brood at around the same time. This is why we should mark everything, so that a control can be made without too much trouble.

Our unit can also serve as well in the event that a hen suddenly deserts her nest, even when we do not become aware of this until several hours later. Parrakeet eggs can endure more than ordinarily supposed. Many eggs are lost, too, because the nesting box was too dry and the young had great difficulty in coming out of the egg, suffocating to death. To prevent this, we should always make sure that the bottom layer of a nest consists of moist turf on which we can spread large wood shavings or other materials like those mentioned earlier. As you can see, humidity plays an important role in the success of a brood. However, occasionally a parrakeet may mess up the nesting material (or completely rid the nest of it) in such a way that the eggs end up in a completely dry nest cavity, as was reported by Dr. Groen in his excellent book *Australian Parrakeets.* Some species can survive this dry condition, but most, unfortunately, will be lost. Consequently, I have tried to mention in the individual descriptions whether or not the

Above and opposite: the Patagonian conure, *Cyanoliseus patagonus,* inhabits Argentina and is very attractive. The people of Argentina often call this bird the "bank-burrowing" parrot because it burrows up to five feet deep into the side of a cliff or a bank to nest. The bird is very sociable, living in colonies and nesting close together.

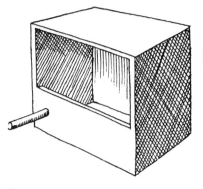

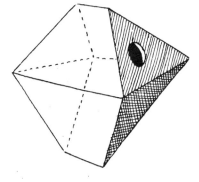

Although different finches' nests are pictured here, there are some small parrots who prefer these small nests on occasion.

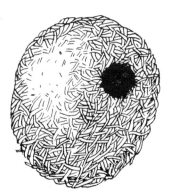

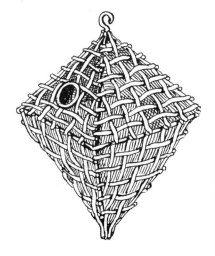

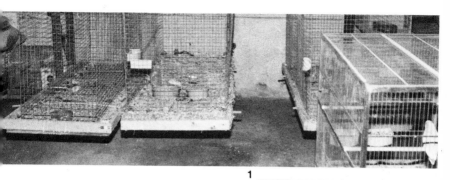

1

2   3

1. Indoor breeding cages are often elevated to avoid mice and rodents. 2. Incubator. 3. The roomier the breeding pen, the healthier the young as they will have plenty of room to exercise.

1. Tui parrakeet, *Brotogeris sanctithomae,* known to be very sensitive to cool temperatures. It must be carefully protected from drafts and cold weather. 2. Nanday conure, *Nandayus nenday.* Few details of nesting habits have been recorded, but it is known that this bird prefers to nest in hollowed-out fence posts, as observed in their natural state in South America. When nesting in captivity, a large nesting box will suffice. 3. The blue-tipped wing coverts of a nanday conure.

2   3

nest cavity must be kept moist. The problem of moving or throwing out the nesting materials can be solved in nesting boxes that have double bottoms by drilling some holes in the upper bottom and placing a dish with water on the second bottom. Firmly pressing some grass sod inside the nesting box may help also, though the first method is superior to the second.

NEST INSPECTION

In order to closely follow the breeding process, regular nest inspections are absolutely necessary. Nest inspection with most tropical and sub-tropical birds is practically impossible, but with parrakeets this is generally a lot easier and, providing we exercise caution, can be carried out without taking too many risks. From the above you might suppose that I am in favor of frequent checks. This is not the case at all; in fact, I feel that our birds should be left alone as much as possible when they are breeding, whether they are finches or parrakeets. Inspections, then, are only justified when they are absolutely necessary, as to remove unfertilized eggs or dead chicks or to remove all eggs if the hen sits on them too irregularly.

An inspection should only take place when the circumstances are favorable. We should never chase a female from her nest for it would not be the first time that a female would refuse to return to her nest. The best time, obviously, is when she has temporarily left her nest to be fed by the male, for example, or to stretch her wings. Sometimes the female may attentively watch your every move while you are making an inspection and then refuse to return to her nest, even though she was not actually chased off it. In such a case it is a blessing to be in the possession of an incubator in which the eggs can be temporarily kept warm; the eggs may not be left in the nest cavity unattended too long (never longer than 24 hours). In this situation we then place a few stones or plaster eggs (which we should always have on hand) into the nest until we are able to determine whether or not the hen intends to return to her nest. We can replace the real eggs quickly at some opportune moment. It would be a rare case where the female does not return to her nest after an inspection has taken place. Nevertheless, I wanted to point out this possibility to you, should this situation ever arise.

THE REARING OF YOUNG PARRAKEETS

I would like to devote a great deal of attention to the rearing of young parrakeets. I am sure you have realized from what you have read so far that we may end up with several different situations and will need to know how to deal with them, since our birds are too valuable to subject to hit or miss treatments.

We must check repeatedly whether or not the female is feeding her young. If not aware of such a situation quickly enough, you will risk losing many valuable young. Young birds cannot go without food very long, which is not so surprising when we consider that they often consume more than their own weight daily. The faster we are aware of a mother bird discontinuing the feeding of her young, the better. Rearing by hand chicks that have just been hatched is virtually impossible if one is not a professional breeder and in the position to be able to feed the chicks every hour. In fact, even those keepers who have this opportunity rarely meet with success. Often after about ten days (if indeed we have managed to keep the chicks alive this long) the young birds die of intestinal problems or other such unpleasantries.

Several authorities feel rather strongly about the current theory that baby birds are fed a so-called "crop milk" for the first few days, and a few universities are researching this theory. It is highly unlikely that it is absolutely necessary for the young to be initially reared on crop milk. Dr. H.D. Groen, in his book *Australian Parrakeets*, says:

"If young birds need crop milk during the first few days to ensure that they will grow up normally, it would follow that the parent bird will begin crop milk production towards the end of the hatching period, when the baby birds can be expected to enter the world. I had an experience with Bourke's Parrots which clearly demonstrates this is not the case. A young Red-Rumped Parrakeet which had just come out of the egg in an incubator was placed in the nest of a Bourke's Parrot. The Bourke's Parrot had at that time not even completed the laying of her own clutch and had been sitting on

The plum-headed parrakeet, *P. cyanocephala,* is a slender parrakeet from India and is very common in European aviaries. It is an ideal bird.

The southern moustached parrakeet, *Psittacula alexandri major,* is from the islands of Lasis and Babi in Indonesia.

1

2

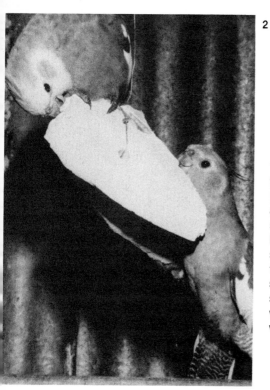

1. Commercial goodies for your bird—found in most petshops. 2. There should always be a cuttlebone supplied for your bird to keep his beak in good shape. 3. Mealworms are taken by some birds so should be offered. 4. Millet spray. 5. A feeding station with protection from the weather.

3

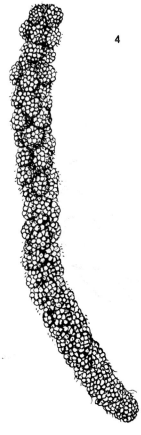

4

5

1

2

3

4

5

1. The scarlet-chested parrot, *Neophema splendida.* 2. A wild pair of scarlet-chested parrots. 3. Turquoise parrots, *Neophema pulchella.* 4. The elegant parrot, *Neophema elegans.* 5. The blue-winged parrot, *Neophema chrysostoma.*

the eggs for two days at the most. Nevertheless, the baby bird was accepted, and some food could already be seen in the baby's crop by that same evening. During the following few days two more Red-Rumped Parrakeets were added to her nest, and all three of them were reared very well and proved to be good and healthy birds. We might assume, therefore, that nothing was lacking in their youth. If the theory regarding crop milk is correct, then the mother bird must have had crop milk available to the babies at a time when her own clutch was no where near hatching."

I had a similar experience with a cactus conure that was given two brown-throated conure babies as foster children. Here, too, the young were fed quite promptly, and long before the cactus conure's own eggs had hatched. In 1965, while I was in Australia for study purposes, I once again had a similar experience, this time with elegant parrots as the foster parents for no less than five turquoise parrot young, when the female elegant parrot was sitting barely four days on six eggs. The correct details with regard to crop milk are obviously not yet known, but one thing is certain: chicks that have just hatched are extremely difficult to rear by hand, regardless of how fast we can get to them after observing that the parents are no longer feeding the young. Usually we notice this just a little too late.

Experience has shown that baby birds need to be about ten days old before we can hope to succeed in rearing them by hand. A thin oatmeal porridge is excellent for the first few days. We serve this warm, otherwise it will simply be refused; by warm we mean lukewarm or body temperature. The food can be fed to the birds with a small European type teaspoon (either plastic or metal), a demitasse spoon, or an eye dropper. Small species can best be fed with a spoon used for stirring mixed drinks, which is even smaller and therefore easier to manipulate. In order to feed them we hold the fledgling in one hand in such a manner that its head is held between thumb and index finger and use the other hand to feed him. After each feeding clean the beak with lukewarm water and a soft cloth (possibly flannel); no spilled food particles should be left on the beak or elsewhere on the bird's body. Sometimes the birds will not accept the food we offer them; in that case, a little sugar added to the concoction can do wonders. Be sure to keep the crop full, but remember that filling it too much is not good either. For the first few days the fledglings will need to be fed every three hours—that is, six times a day. Night feedings are not necessary, as the female does not feed her young during the evening or night either. There is no need to sacrifice your nights!

As I said, about six feedings per day is good, and I have found that the best hours for the feedings are 7 a.m., 10 a.m., 1 p.m., 4 p.m., 7 p.m., and 10 p.m. Some experts advise starting at 8 a.m., but I find that an early feeding in the morning is much better for the birds than ending with a late feeding at night. The baby birds need a lot of rest, and studies have shown that the chicks are hungrier around 10 p.m. than 11 p.m., which is the hour of the last feeding if we start at 8 a.m. Naturally, you are free to choose your own hours, but the feeding times I recommend are those I have found to be best. The first three feedings consist of oatmeal, possibly supplemented with honey, cane sugar, or powdered sugar; the fourth and fifth feedings consist of finely crushed oven-dried bread and baby cereal in addition to the oatmeal, sugar and honey concoction. The sixth feeding should consist of just oatmeal with sugar and honey. The first day the oatmeal should be made with water; in fact, it is best not to use milk for the first five days; after that we can use both milk and water in making our porridge. The second day dried bread and baby cereal may again be offered. After the third day we can add a little raw apple sauce to the menu, sweetened with powdered sugar and/or honey. The apple sauce should not be served too cold either, otherwise it will be refused. On the afternoon of the fourth day, add mashed carrots, served warm; the carrots may not be boiled, however, since too much nutritional value will be lost. We can also mix in finely chopped lettuce and apple. A few drops (never more than two drops for a 2 oz. portion) of cod liver oil or vitamin supplement are highly recommended. Starting with the fifth day, add finely ground egg-shell and a small amount of ground cuttlebone. It is advisable to be stingy with the latter: ½ tsp. divided between the feedings of a single day is sufficient . . . this coincides with Dr. Groen's thinking as well.

It would seem obvious that we prepare the various feedings of each day in the morning, since preparing meals six times a day one at a time would be ridiculous. The prepared food should be kept

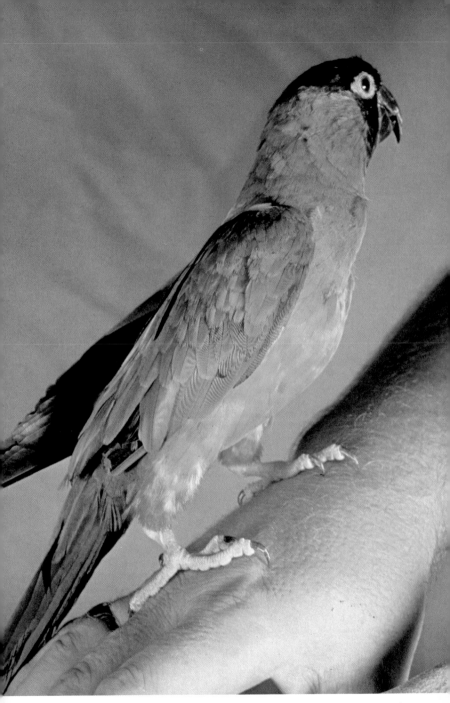

Above and opposite: A nanday conure, *Nandayus nenday*, respond-
ing cooperatively to the author's patient training techniques.

in a cool spot to prevent spoilage. Each meal must be thoroughly heated; baby birds will simply not touch cold food. Theoretically, the fledglings' crops should have emptied after about three hours. However, it is no cause for alarm if this is not the case during the first few days; it simply means that the food you have served them is a trifle too rich. If this happens, we should immediately switch back to a lighter consistency to avoid intestinal and digestive problems; for the next three days it is best to fall back to offering only oatmeal and water; serve this as hot as they will accept it. After ten days we can drop one of the feedings, and after fifteen days four feedings per day will be sufficient, at 8 a.m., 12 noon, 4 p.m., and 10 p.m. During the time that we feed the young birds by hand, we can keep them in a wooden crate 40 cm x 40 cm (16 x 16 inches) placed in a dry, draft-free and warm location (perhaps in the den).

If the bird fancier feeds the birds himself, he may soon feel confident enough to allow the other members of his household to take part in this job. The new little boarders will waste no time in letting you know when they are hungry and wish to be fed. They will soon become accustomed to being fed by hand, and the whole procedure will be accomplished in less and less time. As soon as they see you coming with the food and the teaspoon they will open up their little beaks and it will become child's play.* Still, our project is not yet completed. Soon they will pass into another phase that my wife so aptly calls their "puberty," when they no longer want to remain in their crate and refuse the food we offer them. It is advisable to immediately transfer them to a roomy cage equipped with a few good perches located near the wire so that we can offer their food on the spoon stuck through the wire! Our pets no longer wish to be held, and any attempt to do so anyway may lead to some possibly painful bites. At a later stage this, too, will be in the past because, as you may suppose, birds reared by hand are generally very tame and affectionate. Apart from the menu described above, our young birds should be offered a large variety of *fresh* grass and weed seeds, flattened millet, panicum, and canary seed still on the stem. I purposely say on the stem because the little fledglings will take the stems into their beaks and in this

---

*The eye-dropper should be used only during the first few days because it will soon become clogged when we start serving food of a heavier consistency.

playful manner will learn to eat the seeds off them. However, we will still need to feed them a few meals each day through the wire for the next 14-20 days before we can actually say that our experiment in rearing young parrakeets is a success.

Once the parrakeets are independent, transfer them to a roomier flight so that they can practice their flying to their heart's content. These accommodations may be placed outside, although it should be a suitably warm day before we do this, since a temperature difference that is too great could result in pneumonia or perhaps a cold or similar mishap. Losing your birds at this state of the game due to a minor oversight would be quite a disillusionment for the bird fancier. During the first few weeks we must be sure to check on the birds each night, since it is most important that they spend the nights inside the night shelter. It stands to reason that each aviary should be equipped with a night shelter that is located at a higher level than the flight. As you know, birds instinctively prefer to sit on the highest possible perch when they go to sleep, and this is particularly the case with parrakeets. When satisfied that our foster children are all in the night shelter, close the door that separates the shelter and the flight. At 8 a.m. the next morning open it again. If the weather is unpleasant, the birds should be kept in the night shelter for the first week; this would seem obvious.

As mentioned earlier, birds that have been reared by hand are generally very tame (once they have left the "puberty" phase and have learned to feed themselves) and provide the fancier with a great deal of satisfaction and pleasure. I generally mention in the individual bird descriptions those species that are particularly easy to tame and may even be taught to speak a few words.

Rearing parrakeets by hand could have the disadvantage of ending up with birds that are not suitable for breeding. My personal experience shows that this is often the case with parrots, but certainly not with parrakeets, particularly if we don't turn our parrakeets and parrots into performing artists who know the dictionary from cover to cover and can ride scooters, bikes, and cars! I would like to quote an outstanding expert in this field, Dr. Groen:

"Among my collection of birds there is a male Rosella which has not only successfully bred with a female, but also

Greater Patagonian conure, *Cyanoliseus patagonus,* found in only a few areas in the foothills of the Andes. Once a common species, this bird is now in danger of extinction.

Black-headed caique, *Pionites melanocephala,* from South America. Because many of these birds are kept and bred by the natives of Peru, a great number of them are already tame when imported.

121

1. If the entrance hole is not big enough, the bird will "put his own teeth into it" to accommodate his needs. 2. This cockatiel pen is roomy as it should be. 3. A metal garbage can makes a good nest box because the birds cannot destroy it. This one (for cockatoos) can be used where the summer heat is not a dangerous factor. 4. Incubator.

4

Maroon-bellied conure, *Pyrrhura f. frontalis,* from southeastern Brazil, Uruguay, Paraguay and northern Argentina. This bird was first bred in France in 1919.

Orange-fronted conure, *Aratinga canicularis clarae,* named for the broad orange frontal band, is from western Central America. This bird tames quickly and makes a good pet, but it is difficult to breed in captivity.

helped a great deal in the feeding and rearing of the young. Interesting also, are the experiences of Dr. Overlander (Bad/Honnef/Rhein) who reported that his self reared Eastern Rosellas and Crimson Rosellas bred successfully on a regular basis. This was even the case with birds just one year of age. It is also interesting that he found the females to be very aggressive during the hatching period, especially if there were young in the nest; he said they constantly bit his fingers each time he filled up the seed feeders. After the breeding period, these birds reverted back to their usual tame behavior."

I can add to these interesting facts myself, both from personal experiences and from those of friends. For example, I know of successful breeding results obtained from hand-reared parrakeets of the following species: white-eared conure, barred parrakeet, orange-chinned parrakeet, tui parrakeet, canary-winged parrakeet, nanday conure (4 times); cactus conure (twice); jandaya conure, rose-ringed parrakeet (8 times); plum-headed parrakeet (3 times); and many, many Australian rosella varieties. For those who are interested, we recommend Dr. Groen's book. The birds I mentioned are not Australian species; the fact that Australian parrakeets keep right on breeding regardless of whether they have been reared by hand or not is probably known to most experienced fanciers. While I was in Australia I had ample opportunity to witness the breeding results of countless parrakeets held in captivity and found that there were a great many successful breeding results obtained even with those parrakeets that had been reared with a teaspoon.

Perhaps Dr. Groen intends to add an appendix to his excellent book to cover the cockatiels, which, incidentally, are almost like a cross between the rosellas and cockatoos and really should not be missing in a book on Australian parrakeets, certainly in view of the fact that ornithologists consider the relationship between the two groups to be very close. In this connection I would like to point out that hand-reared cockatiels achieve excellent breeding results, as proved more than once in my own aviaries in the Netherlands, Australia and the U.S.A.

I heartily agree with Dr. Groen's comment that species belonging to the *Neophema* group are extremely difficult to raise by

126

hand. He estimated that only 50% of Bourke's, turquoise, splendid, and elegant parrots that he raised survived and that it is doubtful that breeders elsewhere have had more success, in spite of more optimistic reports they would have us believe. More optimistic magazine articles perhaps should be taken with a grain of salt, particularly since, as Dr. Groen points out, no details on the methods of feeding are given and because the writers do not achieve better results than the 50% level of Dutch breeders. A survey of 82 Australian breeders and 46 American fanciers has convinced me that no more than 50% of hand-reared *Neophema* reach the perch stage.

Let me also say a few words about the so called runts of the brood, which we might come across in a nest of otherwise well-fed fledglings. These are birds that the female has suddenly stopped feeding. Ornithologists are still at a loss to explain this sudden cut-off of food to a particular chick. Even in the wild I have observed several times that one or more babies in a nest of Australian parrakeets were no longer being fed. Needless to say, we must look out for this! I would guess that such behavior on the part of a mother bird is a natural method of curbing the population of a species. This happens with some smaller birds as well, such as Cuban finches (see *All About Finches* by Ian Harman and Dr. Matthew M. Vriends, T.F.H. Publications, Inc.). It could also be that the parent bird instinctively recognizes something wrong with certain baby birds and therefore stops feeding them because they will not grow up into healthy strong adults anyway (natural selection). Whatever the case may be, one thing is certain: we come across this situation with birds held in captivity as well as in the wild. But there is one difference: in captivity the neglected bird is seldom sick or suffering from some other imperfection. It would appear that we have here a definite refusal to feed certain birds, for reasons not yet known to us. Such "black sheep" are best taken from the nest and fed by hand. When the fledgling has been fed well for a few days and has caught up with his brothers and sisters in size, he may be put back into the nest and often will be accepted again by the female, who acts as if nothing was ever amiss.

Finally, I would like to point out that we should not make the various breeding boxes available to our birds until the end of

Crimson rosella, *Platycercus elegans,* about to enter nest area.

Canary-winged parrakeet, *Brotogeris versicolorus,* a very alert, intelligent bird that can be taught to talk easily.

March (I personally set the date at March 25). This period may still be somewhat cold to expect any eggs, but the males need to become accustomed to the females (and vice versa of course), they will still want to thoroughly examine the aviary (especially if they have been housed inside during the winter), their mating rituals such as singing and dancing require some time, etc., so the actual breeding does not take place until the beginning or middle of spring. Generally we can expect the first eggs at the end of April or one week earlier. The individual descriptions of the species will mention the exact time of the breeding season.

This chapter has extensively covered the breeding of parrakeets and the care of young birds. Perhaps you are under the impression that everything is relatively easy, but we must not be too optimistic ... must never forget that we are dealing with *live* material and therefore should keep giving our complete attention to details of housing, feeding, and behavior of our birds. After a while we will become so experienced that we will almost instinctively know when something is not quite right with our birds. However, as long as we have not yet developed this "gift," our daily attention to our pets is a must, with which, no doubt, everyone will agree!

6. Health and Disease

Caribbean brown-throated conure, *Aratinga pertinax aeruginosa*, a very noisy bird that loves to screech. This species travels in pairs or small parties and is often observed traveling to abundant feeding grounds in flocks of a hundred or more birds.

Dusky-headed conure, *Aratinga weddellii*. This is the largest bird in the genus *Aratinga*. In South America, where it occurs, it has been known to serve as a "watch-dog" as well as a pet, warning of the approach of strangers with its noisy chatter.

It is understandable that parrakeets and parrots will become sick if their care and nutrition are in any way lacking. We should pay a lot of attention to giving them the best in housing, feeding, and every other aspect of bird care. If we take the time and trouble to do things right, we should not be faced with all kinds of disasters. Quite often the duration of our bird's sickness is relatively short; therefore, if we are not able to catch the disease quickly it might be too late. For this reason it is important that we familiarize ourselves with our birds by knowing their attitude toward other birds and what constitutes their normal behavior.

If we observe, for example, that a bird quite suddenly is sitting in spots that it normally avoids, we might take this as an indication that something is wrong. If he is making a bigger mess than usual with his food, this can be a bad sign. If he seems to be sitting in a strange way, again we should be alert. When a healthy bird is resting he generally sits on just one foot. If your bird is resting on two (while closing one or both his eyes), then he probably is not feeling 100% healthy.

A birds' plumage should be nice and smooth, his eyes should be bright, and there should not be any dirt hanging from his feet or beak. Speaking of a "smooth" plumage has caused quite a few misunderstandings. When we go to buy a bird, we generally stand very close to the cage; after all, we want to see what we are buying. However, a bird may pass the "smooth plumage test" and still not be a healthy bird. Observe the bird you plan to buy from a moderate distance, preferably in his own "abode" (if possible not in a transportation or observation cage), and you will soon know if the bird is 100% healthy or not.

Many times there are only small indications that imply that a bird is not an entirely healthy specimen. Never wait too long before taking action, such as trying to make sure that something is really wrong while waiting for more definite symptoms. It is better to be too early in taking positive action than too late; later if we should find that our diagnosis was incorrect after all we did not lose anything other than perhaps some time. Being too careful is far better than being nonchalant. If you have doubts about a certain bird, carefully catch him—although this in itself is not too good for parrakeets, especially for the more nervous ones—and place him in a warm (30°-32° C. 86°-88° F.) draft-free area by himself. Since these birds do not like to be confined to small areas, give him a roomy flight if at all possible, such as an attic or shed (possibly their winter home) where you can maintain a constant temperature.

High temperatures make the birds thirsty, and of course they will want to drink more water. This affords the ideal opportunity to add to their water soluble antibiotics that will not cause unpleasant side- or after-effects. Always ask for advice from your local pet shop or bird breeder/dealer regarding medication. We must never withhold food from a sick bird (sadly enough this is done quite frequently). Many of these preparations will stimulate the various glands that give resistance to whatever ails the bird. In addition, fertility is promoted and the shine and color of the bird's plumage are improved. In fact, it is a good idea to add a few drops of such preparations to the water of your birds every once in a while.

It is important to check the perches for all kinds of bacteria and insects on a regular basis since parasites are often the cause of various problems. If you make these inspections every week (every two weeks during the breeding season), being careful not to upset the birds, you will avoid more serious problems. Cleanliness is an absolute must! By paying close attention we can determine whether parasites have gotten into the plumage of our bird, as the feathers will have a brush-like appearance. Take action immediately! Also, if your bird should show signs of losing weight, so that the chestbone sticks out, or if the bird becomes overweight, as evidenced by his difficulty in moving, we must become alert immediately and separate the bird for treatment.

You can also tell if one of your parrakeets is ailing by checking the cloacal (vent) opening. This can be checked without catching the bird. If the bottom part of a female bird's body is swollen, she is probably suffering from egg-binding. If the feathers around the vent are soiled, then we are probably dealing with diarrhea or with an intestinal problem, but of course it may be caused by a more serious disease. That's why it is important that you read a book that deals with parrot diseases.

After a bird has recovered from whatever ailed it, we should not, of course, bring it back immediately to its normal abode. The bird was, after all, in an area where the temperature had been raised as

1. A wild cockatiel, *Nymphicus hollandicus,* found throughout the interior of Australia. 2. An albino cockatiel. This form of the species has been well established. 3. Pied cockatiel. 4. A female cockatiel displays her beautiful crest.

part of the medical treatment, and to bring the bird back to an aviary where the temperature is much cooler would be too much of a shock—our recovered pet would soon be our patient again. Let the temperature in the "sick room" drop gradually until it reaches the normal temperature of the aviary. After that, wait still another few days before letting the bird go back outside. It goes without saying that we should choose a sunny day for this rather than one that is wet and chilly.

As stated before, it is necessary to obtain a book on parrot diseases describing the most common ailments and discomforts of parrakeets. Although we may be obligated to enlist the help of a veterinarian once in a while (especially where expensive parrakeets are concerned), we should be able to act as very good "general practitioners" with the help of *Bird Diseases* by L. Arnall and I. F. Keymer (T.F.H. Publications, Inc., Neptune, N.J.).

And one last word: a parrakeet can die from starvation in 48 hours; naturally this also applies to sick birds. We must try to get the bird to eat and to drink, preferably using his favorite diet. Many birds do not die from their disease, but from starvation!

Feeding by hand

If the bird will not eat by himself, we will have to feed him by hand (teaspoon, eyedropper, etc.). Boil ¼ liter (½ pint) of milk and dissolve a few spoons of honey into it while it is still warm. Beat the yolk of an egg, add a smidgen of salt and add this to the milk too. We may also add 100 milligrams of an antibiotic. Ask your druggist for Terramycin or Aureomycin. This concoction can be stored in the refrigerator, but must be warmed up to 26 °C. (about 80° F.) before it is fed to our little patient.

It can be fed in drops. If we wrap our sick bird in a kitchen towel, there will not be any danger to our eyes and hands nor will he injure or exhaust himself with sudden and unnecessary movements. Place the tip of the dropper (or teaspoon) into the corner of the bird's beak and allow two or three drops of the mixture to fall into his mouth. Be sure not to squirt the food in with the dropper, because it will be a simple matter to get food into the lungs this way and, needless to say, that would not be advisable. After every two or three drops we should wait until our little friend has swallowed his food. Large parrakeet varieties such as the Alexandrine parrakeet can be given 15 drops every four hours, but much less (8-10 drops) for the smaller species. If your bird also has diarrhea, give him some pulverized charcoal with his food or milk with oven-dried bread. Your dealer no doubt has more drugs that should be of help. Be sure, though, not to give these drugs simultaneously with the above formula.

We know either from experience or from what we have already read so far that parrakeets are not often found quenching their thirst at the water dish; in fact, they can do without water for a surprisingly long time. This is why we are presented with a problem when we need to mix drugs with water. The best way to force a bird to drink when he is sick is to place him in a separate, isolated "hospital cage" in an area where we can control the heat. If we place a lamp next to the cage, which we have partially covered with thick towels, we can easily develop a temperature of 30-35° C. (86°-92° F.). The warmth will definitely motivate our patient to drink, and warmth itself is also an excellent medical treatment. We should maintain this temperature for at least 48 hours, and longer if the bird does not show signs of recovering.

Medicines and vitamins should be administered only in small quantities, perhaps on top of a banana or another favorite food, and of course we must be careful to precisely follow the directions.

Aspergillosis

This disease is caused by breathing in spores, particularly of the fungus *Aspergillus fumigatus*. Certain plants, such as those belonging to the genus *Asperula*, can help bring about this fungal infection. Molded bread, seeds, chaff, musty hay, straw, and similar items can also help cause aspergillosis. The spores produce poisonous toxins that damage various tissues such as in the lungs, nostrils, head cavities, air sacs, etc., causing an accumulation of yellow cheese-like pus that of course interferes with deep and clear breathing. The bird loses all interest in food, with the unfortunate result that it becomes seriously weakened. A bird may even shake its head and stretch out its neck regularly, as if trying to dislodge the blockage. No particularly satisfactory remedy has yet been

1. Western rosella, male and female, Pale-headed rosella and Adelaide rosella. 2. Wild cockatiel, *Nymphicus hollandicus.* 3. Twenty-eight parrot, *Barnardius zonarius semitorquatus.* 4. & 5. Blue bonnet, *Psephotus haematogaster.* 6. Red-capped parrot, *Purpureicephalus spurius,* a very shy and easily frightened bird, making it a poor candidate for an aviary. Although the bird does present some difficulties during its adaptation to captivity, it is still a very desirable bird.

2

3   4

5   6

found for clearing up this problem, and it is best to take your bird to a veterinarian.

It is very important that the bird keeper makes it his business to always buy fresh seeds, never old or molded ones. We should not give spilled seed a chance to become moldy; clean the aviary regularly, sweeping up all spilled food. Try to prevent spores from plants from blowing into the aviary in spring and fall, particularly if we live near a lumber yard or lumber business (sawdust) or near any place where hay is stored (we must really beware of wet hay). Whenever a bird has been infected, the entire aviary should be subject to an intensive inspection followed by a thorough cleaning. Finally, we should disinfect everything. Generally, all the birds will need to be killed. Let us hope that veterinarians will soon come up with a drug that can save these birds. The aviary can be sprayed with a solution including 1% copper sulphate before any birds are replaced in the aviary.

Asthma

Fortunately this respiratory problem is rare with parrakeets and parrots, particularly when our birds are housed in a good aviary equipped with a draft- and wind-free night shelter. Birds that are kept indoors suffer from this problem a little more frequently, but all in all it is rare enough so that we need not really worry ourselves about it providing the care of our birds is in order. The first symptoms of asthma are squeaking, difficult breathing, and an overall listlessness. If we act immediately there is a chance that a complete recovery can be achieved. There are several good drugs available on the market (ask your veterinarian for advice; he can prescribe the most recent, and therefore generally the best, drugs available). Place your patient in a bright area where the air is fresh and pure. Give him his usual food, supplemented with fruit, greens, and fresh water.

Be sure you have not mistaken asthma for pneumonia or, more correctly, pneumonitis. With the latter, the lungs are infected and the bird has difficulty in breathing; it makes panting, gasping noises, usually with inhalation but quite often also with exhalation. The droppings are generally green in color, smelly and watery; the bird's plumage is puffed up. Usually a sure sign is that the patient sits with its beak open and also allows its wings to droop. In such a case, of course, we should consult a veterinarian. If for some reason we are unable to do this, we should place our bird in a warm "hospital cage." Cover most of the cage with towels and place a lamp nearby (up to about 2 feet from the front of the cage) to create a constant temperature of 35-37° C. Regularly check on the temperature; a second lamp may be necessary if the first one can't achieve the desired temperature by itself. Maintain this temperature for 48 hours or at least until the bird is completely recovered. Use a broad-spectrum antibiotic that has an effect on a wide range of bacteria. According to Arnall and Keymer, tetracyclines are safe and most likely to be effective, but sometimes sulphadimidine may be useful. Ask your veterinarian. As I mentioned before, a parrakeet will normally drink very little, but the high temperature will change his mind! If he is too sick to drink by himself, we can help him with the use of a dropper. We will need to make fresh formula every day.

Fracture

It may happen that one of your birds breaks his leg or wing, though this is something that we will rarely have to deal with, in contrast to small exotic birds that are constantly having to put up with such problems, particularly when they are housed in an aviary that is too small. The best thing is to consult a veterinarian for a leg or wing fracture, since the bird requires special treatment. When properly set, broken bones will heal quickly and the bird will soon regain the normal use of his leg or wing. For the fancier who wishes to take care of such a matter himself, please refer to the notes in books such as *Bird Diseases* by L. Arnall and I.F. Keymer.

Colds

With inadequate housing and nutrition, any bird can catch a cold. The molting period and even when eggs are being laid can increase the bird's susceptibility to catching a cold; in winter the long nights and short hours of daylight mean that it is indeed *the* time for colds! The cold is caused by a virus that attacks the bird

1. A pair of green rosellas, *Platycerus calendonicus,* female perched on left, male on right. These birds are usually kept in pairs since they are not congenial with other birds. 2. The crimson rosella, *Platycercus elegans.* 3. Blue rosella, or pale-headed rosella, *Platycercus adscitus palliceps,* a very hardy breed from northeastern Australia. In captivity, a nest box filled with a layer of sawdust will be readily accepted for nesting as a substitute for a hollow in a tree, which is preferred for nesting in the wild.

when he has the least resistance. He sneezes, has watery eyes, puffed up feathers, and is listless. The bird should be isolated from the other aviary inmates and placed in our hospital cage, as heat is the main remedy. We recommend administering sulfa drugs (ask your druggist). If it just has a chill, the bird should recover quickly, but we should not return him to the aviary until he is completely recovered. When birds are brought inside from outdoor quarters they should not be put outside again until spring.

Coccidiosis

This is a parasitic disease of the intestine that sets up inflammation; it is fortunately rare with parrots and parrakeets, especially with birds kept in cages. Birds that are kept in an aviary may be infected by wild birds that land on or near the aviary, but also when they come in contact with fowl-type birds (such as chickens, pheasants, peacocks, etc.). Usually, however, the disease is brought into the aviary by the infected droppings of sparrows, starlings, and the like.

As soon as we notice that a bird has been infected, we need to act immediately. All sick birds must be caught and placed in individual hospital cages and treated with care. We must act fast because this disease is extremely contagious and can infect the whole population in less than no time. Sick birds quickly lose weight and have a bloody diarrhea. Fortunately sulfa drugs (sulphadimidine, sulphaquinoxaline) and antibiotics will get coccidiosis under control very fast. Here again it is best to consult a veterinarian (the monetary value of our birds alone is enough to warrant a visit to the vet) because playing doctor ourselves rarely clears up the problem and usually makes things worse. We need to disinfect the aviary; there are several excellent disinfectants to choose from, and no doubt your local pet store will be happy to help you make a choice.

Coccidia are protozoan (one-celled) parasites of different types. The oocytes or cysts of the genus *Eimeria* that come within reach of the bird via the droppings are the cause of the infection. If the cage is not kept immaculately clean and droppings remain within reach of the sick bird, he may re-infect himself and thereby intensify the infection.

Constipation

Birds that are housed in an area that is too small have a greater tendency to be afflicted with this ailment. Insufficient movement, food that is too rich, and eating too much (which is often done by birds that are housed in quarters that are too tight) are also causes. If the droppings are expelled with some difficulty and are dry, large, and hard, we can assume our bird is constipated. First we should consider whether the bird's menu is in order; adding greens, fruit, etc. is advisable, as is adding some crystals of Epsom or Glauber salt in the drinking water. It is more effective to put salts into the beak with a medicine dropper. Although these are rather old fashioned treatments, they seem to work very well. We can also make use of an oily laxative (obtainable at any good drug store); a small amount dissolved in the drinking water or administered with a dropper can bring about a noticeable improvement. Rape seed rubbed in grease can also do wonders.

Diarrhea

When suffering from diarrhea, our birds have a dull look to their eyes. They are listless, exhausted, and have thin, slimy, foul-smelling droppings that are generally yellow-green or white in color. Quite often the vent is inflamed and the feathers around it are soiled. Diarrhea can occur when their nutritional requirements are not met; drinking and bathing water are too cold; greens, eggs, and strengthening foods are too wet; and as the result of a severe temperature change. Withhold all greens and seeds rich in oil; offer maw seeds and other binding seeds instead. Mix penicillin into the drinking water according to the directions and place the bird in a warm and draft-free area. Clean the vent regularly with lukewarm water in which we have dissolved a little mild disinfectant. A veterinarian will prescribe sulfa drugs.

Egg Binding

When nesting places, housing space, food, and such are not as they should be, we can count on having one or more females that will develop a problem with the laying of their eggs during the breeding season. If a female is overweight or if she is exposed to

An elegant pied or harlequin cockatiel. The pied cockatiel is not common, especially one marked as evenly as the one pictured here.

A beautiful pair of white cockatiels, *Nymphicus hollandicus*. Considering their flight habits, cockatiels do best in a large aviary; their docile disposition allows them to be kept in a mixed collection.

draft and cold at the time she expects her eggs, egg binding will occur. The lack of certain minerals in her diet can also cause her eggs to have no or insufficient shells, so that it is difficult to expel them; in some cases this may even lead to a rupture in the oviduct. Any birds that we wish to breed will need to be kept in very good health.

The symptoms of a bird suffering from egg binding are simple to recognize. She has puffed up feathers, usually sits on the ground (often in a corner on the floor of the aviary), the eyes are half shut, and the vent is swollen and sore. We should pick her up and place her in a very warm spot in a hospital cage without perches, where we can create high temperatures of about 90 degrees. A little olive or mineral oil placed in the cloaca with a small brush will do wonders. Half a teaspoon of glycerine dissolved in the drinking water can also bring relief. The warmth will give her back control of her muscles, and usually her egg will be laid within a few hours. If this is not the case, we will need to administer more olive oil to her cloaca and hold her above a container with boiling water. Only do the latter when she has not been able to lay her egg after one or two attempts with the olive oil. Obviously we should handle the bird as little as possible to avoid breaking the egg inside her . . . that will cause her death, although a veterinarian (*only* a veterinarian) with surgical forceps can break an egg in the cloaca when other treatments have not worked and will remove as much as possible of the bits and pieces of the egg in the cloaca. The female will not be suitable for further breeding if she has chronic egg binding. A hen may become egg bound from chill when the temperature has dropped below 45° F., the grit lacks calcium, or the food is not what it should be.

Blocked crop or Impaction of the crop

A blocked crop will occur once in a while with young birds, though seldom with older ones, when they have swallowed something. Sometimes this may cause pressure on the windpipe, causing the bird to suffocate. When a situation exists where there is a definite possibility that a bird may choke, it will be quite apparent: the crop will be swollen and breathing difficult. Wrap the patient in a towel and drop a little olive oil in his crop, carefully massaging the mass that is blocking the crop upward toward the beak. Thread and the like can usually be removed by opening the bill as wide as possible and grasping the object with a pair of tweezers. In serious cases it will be unavoidable for the veterinarian to do minor surgery.

Mites, lice, etc.

Birds infested with mites or lice are rather restless, and their movements and posture betray their itchiness. Their general state of good health deteriorates. Chlorosis, anemia, gluttony, inflammations, bare spots, and a great many infectious diseases can follow as a result of insect and parasite bites. The female that is sitting on eggs or has young in the nest may desert them. Young birds still in the nest that are attacked at night by red mites and the like usually die. The most common parasites are red mites (a real source of trouble!), feather mites, mosquitoes and lice. Several of these species will come at night in great numbers, sit on the birds, and suck their blood. During the day they hide in corners, cracks, etc. The only way to exterminate these pests and avoid recurring visits is a regular and careful control of cleanliness. Inspect the nesting boxes at night. If you see any insects, use a small amount of a safe commercial spray, following the instructions on the label. Effective acaricides are malathion and gamma benzene hexachloride for red mites and iodine, antihistamines and sulphur ointment for feather mites. In any event, never use DDT, HCH, Lindane, or any other poisonous products.

Personal Hygiene

It is of the utmost importance that anyone who takes care of sick birds or comes into contact with them is aware of the fact that he can easily be a carrier of the disease if he does not thoroughly wash his hands after every treatment or contact with a sick bird. I was dismayed when I observed how infrequently this practice was adhered to. If our birds should have psittacosis or another contagious disease and we merely went from one patient to the next one, we would soon make things a lot worse than they already were. Incidentally, the proper name for psittacosis is actually or-

The red-rumped parrakeet, *Psephotus haematonotus,* has a call that has been described as sounding almost song-like.

The cockatiel is a definite favorite of aviculturists. This bird can actually become affectionate.

nithosis, but most people still know it as "parrot fever." It may still rear its ugly head from time to time but generally belongs to the past. If you diagnose a case of ornithosis, a vet should be consulted immediately. It is only when we are meticulous both with ourselves and our birds that we can avoid disease in our birds. If we are in the habit of wearing rubber gloves for these treatments, we must disinfect the gloves each time we have handled a sick bird.

One final piece of advice. It is clear that in this last chapter I have not even come close to touching on all the diseases and afflictions that may trouble your birds. Therefore, I advise every bird fancier to equip himself with a good book on the subject of bird diseases. We highly recommend *Bird Diseases* by Drs. L. Arnall and I.F. Keymer, an introduction to the study of birds in health and disease, especially concerning birds in captivity.

7. Description of the Species

Cockatiel embryo.

Nine days old.

Four days old.

Six days (left) and nine days (right).

Six days old.

Ten days old.

Seven days old.

Twelve days old.

Thirteen days old.

Nineteen days old.

Fourteen days old.

A family portrait: 21, 19 and 17 days old from left to right.

Fifteen days old.

Twenty days old.

Seventeen days old.

Twenty-two days old.

GROUP I:
AMERICAN PARRAKEETS (CONURES)

Some very well known parakeet species are found in the Americas, such as the green-rumped parrotlet (*Forpus passerina*) and the monk parrakeet (*Myiopsitta monachus*). As you can see, this group consists of some extremely varied types but the genera are known for the fairly broad cere at the base of the beak. It is also noteworthy that their fairly sturdy beaks are never red in color, the most common colors being black and light flesh.

The shape of the tail warrants comments. Birds belonging to this group fall into one of two categories: firstly, there are those with a short tail that becomes narrower at either the root or the tip; and secondly, there are those that stand out because of their long tail, such as *Ara*. All species belonging to the genus *Psittacula* have tails that are very short; on the other hand, species of *Aratinga* (previously known as the genus *Conurus*), of which the well known jandaya conure (*A. jandaya*) and the brown-throated conure (*A. pertinax*) are members, have a slender tail. Nevertheless, we will soon see that the construction of the tail of birds in this group follows the two possibilities described before: either they are more sharply narrowed toward the tip of the tail or they are narrower at the root of the tail than in other parrakeet groups.

Practically all species of this group (excluding those of a few more normal genera) have a clearly defined eye-ring. This eye-ring can be very helpful in determining the sex outside the breeding season, as females generally have a narrower ring than the males.

The sides of the head are generally naked or partially covered with small feathers. We should, therefore, not be misled into thinking that we are dealing with a sick bird or one that is molting. These birds, which are relatively simple to breed, are not bothered by mites or other vermin, which might be thought to be the cause of the bare spots; these are merely a characteristic of birds in this group.

Ornithologists recognize approximately 125 different species and subspecies in this group. Generally speaking, they can be found in most of South America; obviously I will cover only the most important members. Quite frequently throughout this book we will come across a species, genus, or group that is identified by more than just one name. This is due to the fact that a few experts in the field are currently reviewing the scientific naming and grouping structure, and we felt it wise to include both the old and the new names in connection with possible further study on the part of the reader.

The members of the conure group are nice, peaceful birds that soon become accustomed to their keeper and often enjoy a flourishing friendship with him. Even in the wild they have a sweet nature and will seldom be seen fighting with each other. In the wild they live together in groups of twenty to thirty birds . . . even during the mating season! This in itself illustrates a peace-loving nature. Because of their fast and beautiful flight, it would be wise to house them only in very large aviaries. The aviculturist has learned from experience that the minimum measurements of an aviary should be 3 x 2½ x 3 meters (9 x 7½ x 9 feet). The night shelter also should not be too small; 2 x 3 x 3 meters (6 x 9 x 9 feet) would be ideal. You will see that the shelter and flight have identical height measurements. As mentioned in one of the previous chapters, it might be wise to build the shelter just a little taller than the flight, since birds like to sleep at the highest possible level. In this way we can more or less force the birds to spend the night in the shelter. This is particularly important when cold winter weather arrives.

The birds of the conure group will rarely be found on the ground due to their somewhat plump build that makes it difficult for them to fly upward; they are rather helpless, then, when on the ground. Their song, unfortunately, is not pleasant to hear and is often mere screaming. They feed on fruit (pears, cherries, bananas, pineapples cut in small pieces, apples, and peanuts and other nuts) and seeds (even when kept in an aviary they should be provided with rice and corn on a daily basis); some even eat live foods (mealworms, white worms, ant-eggs, and such). They have even been known to attack smaller species of birds during migrations in the fall and eat them. It follows that in order not to take any chances, we should not place them with smaller birds. Supplement their diet with white bread, egg, honey, and universal food.

Only one species builds a traditional type nest in trees or high shrubbery. The rest of the species nestle in tree hollows (the nest-

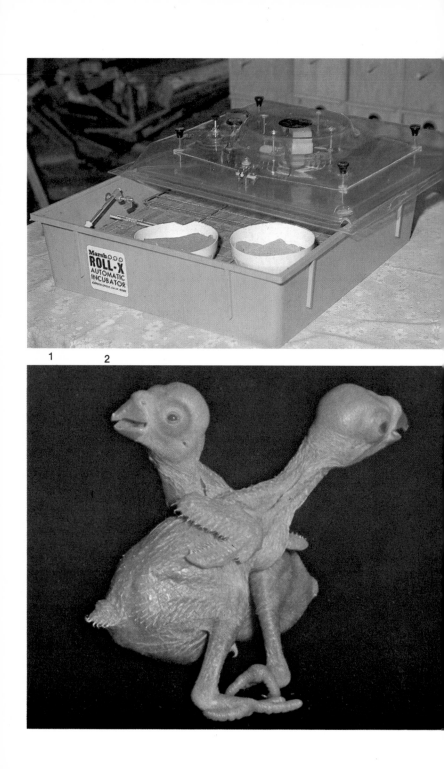

1   2

3

1. An automatic incubator. The eggs are placed in the bowls a few days before hatching to keep the newly hatched chicks more confined in the incubator. 2. Young lutino ringnecks, *Psittacula krameri manillensis.* 3. Candling a grass parrakeet egg. 4. This young cockatiel lutino is only about six days old.

4

ing box would be the counterpart in the aviary) or in rock crevices (in the aviary we would imitate this with a half-open nesting box).

GENUS *FORPUS* (PREVIOUSLY *PSITTACULA)*

I was undecided for a while whether or not to include this group in with the parrakeets, because they are really considered parrots, particularly by bird fanciers; they are more-or-less South America's answer to the lovebirds of Africa, which are considered to be little parrots. However, the *Forpus* species are considerably smaller in build, so that I cannot see any reason to view these as miniature lovebirds. In fact, I see them as miniature Amazon parrots.

Due to their long and sharply tapered wings, their flight is skillful and fast. When these birds are nesting, their wings lie almost half way across on their rounded-off tails. Their individual tail feathers are very pointed. It is a simple matter to determine their sex, because the females lack all bright colors except green.

Ornithologists recognize 20 different members in this genus, consisting of 5 species with about 20 subspecies. Their natural habitat is tropical Central and South America. Various species, I feel, are closely related to the plum-headed parrakeet (see under the description of this bird).

Most of the birds offered for sale in this country have been imported; therefore, it is of the utmost importance that a correct acclimation procedure be followed. In order to do this we cannot place them in an outside aviary with other birds for a few weeks, but rather should place them inside in a light, heated area, preferably sunny, so that they become adjusted to the temperature and food differences. Getting them slowly accustomed to live food during the acclimation period is most sensible; never give more than three mealworms per bird per day; this quantity can be somewhat increased at a later date. It is certainly noteworthy that, once they have become accustomed to local weather and food, they are extremely hardy birds and can even stay outside during the winter, providing they have access to a wind- and rain-free night shelter. Many species kept by fanciers have repeatedly reared broods successfully.

Green-rumped Parrotlet (*Forpus passerinus* or *Psittacula passerina passerina*

Distribution: Guyana, Surinam, Venezuela, Trinidad, and Colombia.

Male: Beautiful ultramarine blue breast and wings. Head, back, rump, and tail typical parrot-green. Underparts deep reddish yellow to yellowish brown. Eyes grayish brown. Light, somewhat flesh-colored beak, ash-gray at its root.

Female: Generally a brighter green, the breast is grass-green, though some birds are surprisingly light.

Length: 12 cm (4 4/5 inches); wings: 8.2 cm (3¼ inches); tail: 3¼ cm (1 1/5 inches).

Offspring: Initially look much like the mother. The males can soon be identified by the blue glow on their wings (usually visible about two weeks after they first fly out), although of course this is not yet as bright as in adult males. Blue feathers can be seen glowing through the green ones on the back and sometimes on the tail as well; the breast shows this soonest, however.

Particulars: Their call is sharp and loud and can be heard from quite a distance. The peeping sound somewhat resembles that of the sparrow. Their contact with each other is similar to that of the titmouse; in the presence of danger, they constantly warn each other. There is indeed a close bond between these birds. They live in small troops except during the breeding season. Outside of the breeding season, they often go on hunting expeditions together and can do quite a lot of damage to fruit orchards (tamarinds, pears, etc.). These birds use the deserted nests of other birds, such as the red oven bird (*Turnarius rutus*), a small tropical bird seldom found among any individual's collection.

The green-rumped parrotlet nests twice a year in the wild and even three times per year in the aviary. Usually the first brood is started quite late in the year, about August or September, but if we give them a helping hand we can persuade them to start a few months earlier. The breeding seems to take care of itself quite well, as long as we have them inside, because during the winter several factors would come into play that could easily ruin good breeding results.

In recent years, many of these birds have become available on the market. Little wonder, since they are very nice birds, though

This nest box is suitable for a turquoise parrot.

Eggs of turquoise parrot, *Neophema pulchella,* in a nest box; incubation lasts about twenty days.

they do have one drawback: they tend to remain timid and nervous with their keeper and other members of the household for quite a long time. This characteristic is not found in their counterparts in the wild, however, which curiously enough are quite bold and pert. We want to emphasize the fact that the green-rumped parrotlet should not be placed with other species if we wish to avoid possible unpleasantries.

Females in the wild lay about four eggs, whereas those in aviaries may lay as many as eight, deposited on alternate days. The egg measure 17-20 mm x 14-15½ mm. Only the female sits on the eggs, and for a period of about three weeks. The male feeds her faithfully, and later the young as well, which grow rapidly and at around four days old are already covered with a thick coat of yellowish-white nest down. The fledglings leave the nest at about one month, but will continue to be fed by the parents for at least another fourteen days. We would like to point out the importance of separating the fledglings from the parents once the chicks have become independent. This will also allow and encourage the parents to start on the next brood. Breeding results are generally quite successful. For example, in the breeding season of 1957 my green-rumped parrotlet pair presented me with eleven young in two broods; in 1962 this same couple repeated the effort and produced some 13 young in two broods, of which 12 lived; one was killed in an accident just three days after leaving the nest. In Florida in 1969, a new couple of mine achieved breeding results.

The green-rumped parrotlet of Venezuela (*Forpus passerinus viridissimus*) is primarily green, lighter on the head and abdomen. The rump is a considerably brighter green. A vague turquoise color can be seen shining through the feathers of the wings. The beak is flesh-colored. Another well known *Forpus* is the blue-winged parrotlet, *Forpus xanthopterygius flavissimus,* from the northeastern area of Brazil. Both wings and rump display a cobalt blue, as well as some blue in the neck and pale green on the throat. The female is devoid of any blue. The blue-winged dwarf parrotlet (*Forpus passerinus vividus*) lives in the south of Brazil to Paraguay and northeastern Argentina. This bright green little bird has a very pointed tail. The underparts are pale green in contrast to the rich deep green on its head. The beak is grayish in color. There are several cobalt blue markings on the male, but the female does not have these and her green is also less bright.

Forpus passerinus has several other subspecies, but they are rarely seen on the market. For the sake of completeness, however, we will list the most important ones: *Forpus passerinus spengeli* (Colombia); *Forpus passerinus cyanophanes* (Colombia); *Forpus passerinus cyanochlorus* (northwest Brazil); *Forpus passerinus deliciosus* (below the Amazon River); *Forpus passerinus crassirostris* (Peru and western Brazil); *Forpus passerinus flavescens* (Bolivia).

A better known bird is the Mexican parrotlet (*Forpus cyanopygius cyanopygius*), an inhabitant of western Mexico. The rump, lower back, part of the wings, and even the inside of the wings are blue; the female has no blue coloring. Both sexes are a bright greenish yellow on the forehead. Two other subspecies are *Forpus cyanopygius pallidus* from northwestern Mexico and *Forpus cyanopygius insularis* from the western-most part of Mexico and the Tres Marias Islands.

The spectacled parrotlet (*Forpus conspicillatus caucae*), from western Colombia is somewhat larger than the species described so far. Another subspecies, *Forpus conspicillatus conspicillatus*, inhabits northern Colombia, but there are only minor coloring differences to set these two birds apart; the last named subspecies is generally darker in coloring. The spectacled parrotlet has some deep blue in the rump and wings; the rest of the body is green, lighter on the underside, and strikingly light green under the eyes. The female has no blue on rump and wings.

Not too well known in Europe but quite common in Peru is the Pacific parrotlet (*Forpus coelestis*), which to the best of my knowledge was first bred by Mrs. Boorer from London. This bird comes from the tropical areas of western South America. The underside of the wings are a beautiful cobalt blue, and there is also quite a lot of blue on rump and upper wing coverts and also a tinge of blue around the eyes. The back is grayish green, the balance of the body green. A second species is quite common in the north of Peru and is kept by aviculturists, namely *Forpus xanthops* or the yellow-faced parrotlet.

All of the above-mentioned birds are not really parrakeets, but ornithologically speaking do not really belong in the parrot group either. They require the same care as the green-rumped parrotlet.

Budgerigar, *Melopsittacus undulatus,* a very common bird from Australia and one of the most familiar cage birds. This species has produced a wider range of colors than any other.

The mulga parrot, *Psephotus varius,* also called the many-colored parrakeet, is found in the southern interior of Australia. Special care in both the diet and the handling of this bird is necessary to establish it in captivity. Once adapted to captivity, it becomes quite tame and well-suited to life in an aviary.

GENUS *MYIOPSITTA (MYIOPSITTACUS)*

The birds belonging to this genus are very interesting indeed, because they build rather crude, loosely woven nests. For nesting materials they use branches and twigs, so we need to supply them with these in the aviary. They make their nests in trees, and in the aviary we generally do not need to supply them with nesting boxes. They are very attractive when kept in a roomy aviary.

Ornithologists recognize only one species and four subspecies, all of which look very much alike with only minimal differences between them. Only the bird described below is offered for sale on the market.

Monk Parrakeet (*Myiopsitta monachus*)

Distribution: South America. A resident population introduced into southeastern New York, New Jersey, and Connecticut; nests have been recorded also from Massachusetts, Virginia and Florida.

Male: Forehead, crown, and occiput grayish blue; cheeks, throat, and lores pale gray. Back of head, neck, back, rump, wings, and tail are parrot-green.

Female: Generally somewhat lighter in color, but in many instances there is almost no difference at all. The young birds are a brighter green initially.

Length: 30 cm (12 inches); wings: 12-15 cm (4 4/5 inches); tail: 14 cm (4 3/5 inches).

Particulars: Due to their peaceful and pleasant nature, these birds can be tamed quite readily. Although their screaming may be a little loud for keeping them in the house, their reputation as screamers is exaggerated. One of the disadvantages of keeping them in an aviary is the nest that they build; although its construction is interesting enough, it takes up quite a lot of space and they will be unlikely to breed unless their housing has very generous dimensions and shrubbery is plentiful, because their bullet-shaped nest is very large. We once saw in a zoo a monk parrakeet's nest that had a diameter of 75 cm (30 inches). Ornithologist and author Karl Neunzig wrote in his book *Fremdlandische Stubenvogel,* which appeared in Amsterdam in 1968 but really dated from 1921, about a nest that had a diameter of 1.15 meters (3½ feet). Needless to say, such nest-building is fascinating. There is an entrance to the nest that is completely protected with a little portico; the parents often sit here to watch the world go by and to keep a lookout for possible danger (using it as a guard post). The nest itself consists of two rooms. The eggs are hatched in the back room, while the room that leads to the portico could be considered a living room since the parents spend most of their time here, including the night. When the young are bigger, they, too, will move into the living room so that the female can start laying a new clutch.

The breeding season takes place mostly in October and the winter months.* If possible, we should discourage winter breeding, although we know of successful cases. However, these fanciers generally had access to heated areas in which to house their birds. Should you allow your birds to breed in the winter, you would need to provide them with extra food in the form of hard boiled eggs and white bread soaked in water or milk. This food, of course, should also be extended during their "normal" breeding season, that is, October and November.

The female builds the nest by herself and cleans and extends it each year, so that it is often used for several years, perhaps even five or more. She sits on some four to eight eggs that measure 27½ x 20½ mm. The male does not help with these chores in the wild either.

Their food requirements consist of oats, hemp (not too much), corn, sunflower seeds, panicum millet, canary seed, fruit, young and fresh buds and twigs, greens (lettuce, endive, chickweed, chicory, sprouts, spinach, etc.), cuttlebone, and grit.

Because of their sometimes deafening scream, it is not always easy to breed other parrakeet species nearby, as I have noticed that their screaming makes other birds nervous. I can also imagine that your spouse would not be too thrilled to have to listen to this occasional screaming if he or she is home during the day. It might be advisable to ask your neighbors if they have any objections before you buy a pair of monk parrakeets. Obviously, not every neighbor is a bird enthusiast! Notwithstanding their occasionally annoying

*Seasons refer to those of the northern hemisphere; south of the equator seasons are reversed—January is summer, July winter, etc.

The sun conure, *Aratinga solstitialis,* has more yellow in the wings than the jandaya conure.

The jandaya conure, *Aratinga jandaya,* is one of the favorites in aviculture. The bird is vividly colorful but quite expensive.

screaming, several bird fanciers have successfully bred this bird. They were not only rewarded with several beautiful young, but have even managed to create a blue variation that can be admired or purchased in better pet shops for not too enormous amounts of money.

These birds can remain outside during the winter, providing they have access to a draft-free night shelter. It is imperative that this species be given fruit during the breeding season. In fact, many fanciers allow the male to fly freely in the immediate area during the breeding season so that he can enthusiastically seek out all kinds of goodies without doing all that much damage to plants and shrubbery as claimed by some dreadfully exaggerating authors. Another advantage of these birds is that they can be very easily acclimated. I have also seen several birds that could clearly speak a few words.

The four subspecies mentioned earlier are: *Myiopsitta monachus luchsi; Myiopsitta monachus cotorra; Myiopsitta monachus calita;* and *Myiopsitta monachus monachus.*

GENUS *PYRRHURA*

Members of this genus are noted for their slender bodies and extremely long, attractively constructed tails that are usually partially or completely reddish brown on the underside. The wings are also long and pointed. Ornithologists recognize about forty species and subspecies that inhabit South America and one species which lives in Central America.

Their song has a screeching quality that is far from pleasant to the ear; nevertheless, they can be found among various bird collections today. It is extremely difficult to determine their sex, so it is essential for you to make arrangements with the seller to be allowed to exchange one of the birds should they not form a true pair. The females lay only a small clutch, generally just two eggs, sometimes four. This is the case in both the wild and in the aviary.

Maroon-bellied conure (*Pyrrhura frontalis frontalis*)
Distribution: Southeastern Brazil.
Male: Green on top and back; clearly visible red stripe on the

174

head; the area around the eye is brownish yellow. This bird also has some blue on the wings, which are otherwise green; the tail is reddish brown.

Female: The female is identical to the male in coloring; perhaps the blue in her wings is a little less bright, but one would need to be quite an expert to be able to distinguish this, and often there is no difference at all anyway. This is why we stress once again that you must obtain a written agreement from the dealer allowing you to exchange one of the birds should they prove to be of the same sex. We stress this because all too often bird fanciers are deceived and receive birds of the same sex, or even birds of two related but not identical species, for their hard-earned money. Go only to reputable dealers when you wish to buy birds; any bird-fanciers club is sure to be able to recommend dealers in your area.

Length: 23 cm (9 1/5 inches), sometimes 25-27 cm (10-11 inches); wings about 13 cm (5 1/5 inches); tail 13 cm (5 1/5 inches).

Particulars: This bird can be kept in either a large aviary or a roomy cage. When they first arrive, they are restless and sometimes quite wild, constantly flying against the bars or wire. It is therefore important that recently arrived birds are housed in a roomy aviary with lots of shrubbery and left alone so that the other aviary inhabitants can make them feel at home. Once they become accustomed to captivity and the food, they will become very affectionate and will very likely soon come to take some delicious morsel out of your hand. Once accustomed to the food and their surroundings, they can also be kept in a roomy cage. However, if we wish them to breed, they almost must be kept in an aviary, and this time without any other birds. Other data with regard to breeding and care are identical to that for the white-eared conure, so the interested reader is referred to the description of that species. I would like to note here, however, that the young will grow up much healthier when the parents are offered soaked corn.

Cross-breeding has taken place between a male white-eared conure and a female maroon-bellied conure. Some aviculturists have also succeeded breeding the two species, but with the sexes switched around. For the sake of retaining as much purity in the species as possible, I am not exactly a strong supporter of these cross-breeding attempts, particularly because the differences between

175

Two hooded parrakeets, *Psephotus chrysopterygius dissimilis;* the male is the lower bird. One difficulty in breeding these birds is that they insist on nesting during winter months. As long as they are willing to accept a nest box in a heated area, there shouldn't be any problem protecting the young against the cold.

the various members of the genus *Pyrrhura* are so slight already. All of them are pretty much the same size, all have rather open and clearly visible nostrils, all have long tails that are a vague red on the underside and green on the top, and all have markings on the breast. Almost all of the species have a breast that is yellow with a sprinkling of either light or dark brown feathers. Many of them have some blue in the wings and red in the under tail-coverts. All have a black beak, and some have a horn-colored cere.

The spots on the cheeks generally vary between the species, but even experienced aviculturists feel the entire genus tends to be confusing, and I must admit I wholeheartedly agree. Since there is very little literature available on these undoubtedly beautiful birds, I felt it a good idea to devote a few extra words to them. Less well known is the subspecies *Pyrrhura frontalis chiripepe* from eastern Salta and Paraguay. What stands out about this sub-species is the dark "ears." There is quite a lot of red on the belly as well as under the tail. The beak is bordered by a narrow brown band.

Very closely related, and as far as I know never yet bred in captivity, is *Pyrrhura frontalis kriegi.* This subspecies, which lives in Brazil, has a somewhat smaller tail than *chiripepe,* has a green back, a tinge of blue in the wings, and red on the tail. The underside of the tail is bright red. There is also some bright red on the abdomen of this bird, but the yellow pointed marking on the breast makes this bird really gorgeous. There is a brown line above the nostrils and the bill is grayish black.

The blue-throated conure (*Pyrrhura cruentata*) is a little better known and inhabits the coastal states of Brazil. I believe this is the largest of the group, and it is primarily green in color. There is some blue in the lesser and middle wing-coverts, random auburn markings on the abdomen, some rust-colored feathers, some feathers in the under tail-coverts are rather dull, a few vague blue colors in the breast, chestnut "ears," and some orange spots on the breast, throat, neck, and flanks. The beak is blackish.

The pearly conure (*Pyrrhura perlata perlata*) is also fairly well known as a cage and aviary bird in Brazil, though I have also seen them in Peru and Argentina. The interesting thing about this bird is that man still has not determined exactly where in South America this bird can be found naturally, but considering that there are two other subspecies (*Pyrrhura perlata coerulescens* and *Pyrrhura perlata anerythra*), they must inhabit a fairly large region, because otherwise these subspecies which reveal minor differences would not have been established by ornithologists. The pearly conure is smaller than the blue-throated conure and *Pyrrhura frontalis chiripepe*. It is primarily green with some blue in the wings, red in the lower tail-coverts and the abdomen, and darker on the head. The "ears" are a dull brown, and vague blue colors glow through the feathers of the forehead, neck, cheeks, breast, and flanks. The feathers around the anus and some of the tail feathers also have blue colors among them. This blue is quite a lot darker than the other blue shades that appear elsewhere on the body of this bird.

White-eared conure (*Pyrrhura leucotis leucotis*)

Distribution: Coastal states of Brazil.

Male: The head is dark brown, as is the area around the beak and the sides of the face. This bird has a striking grayish white line by the ears and a reddish brown crown. Neck and throat are bright blue changing to green. Black and white semi-circles following the shape of the feathers run cross-wise from the throat down almost to the abdomen. The green color changes to a reddish brown marking on the belly. The tail is long and slender and brownish red. The wings are blue and green. Eyes brownish red, feet black, beak grayish black, and with a yellowish white cere.

Female: Practically identical to the male; perhaps the colors are not as distinct.

Length: 23 cm (9 1/5 inches); wings 11-12 cm (4 2/5-4 4/5 inches); tail 10-13 cm (4-5 1/5 inches).

Particulars: White-eared conures are pleasant birds that can be tamed quite easily. They are currently very popular. The female lays only about two eggs, upon which only she sits. A closed nesting box (possibly of beech) that measures 25x35 cm (10x14 inches), with an opening about 6 cm (2 2/5 inches) in diameter, would be ideal.

Once the young birds have hatched, we highly recommend that you supplement the menu with soaked stale white bread, cooked corn, sunflower seeds, boiled potatoes, and a little hemp and oats.

1. Bourke's parrot, *Neophema bourkii,* pied variety. A peaceful bird suited for a medium sized aviary with a mixed collection. 2. Frontal view of a pied Bourke's parrot. 3. A yellow Bourke's parrot. Contrary to common belief, this bird is a very common species in the wild. The reason it was thought to be so rare is because it inhabits only the sparsely populated areas of southern and central Australia.

181

1. Australian king parrot. 2. Green-winged king parrot. 3. Scarlet chested parrakeet. 4. Cockatiel. 5. Red-capped parrakeet. 6. Princess parrot.

5

6

1

1. Pairs of Stanley rosellas should be housed separately during breeding periods. 2. A pair of Adelaide rosellas, *Platycercus adelaide.* It is speculated that this species may have originated from the natural cross-breeding of the pennant (crimson) rosella and the yellow parrakeet *(Platycercus flaveolus).*

2

3. The Stanley rosella, *Platycercus icterotis xanthogenys*, prefers a diet of plain canary seed, hulled oats, crushed corn and leafy greens. Grit and cuttlefish should also be supplied. 4. A pair of Adelaide rosellas.

3

4

Occasionally we should give them a salt block, cuttlebone, grit, and ground egg shells. In order to completely spoil them, we could give them sliced carrots once a week. They should be offered a variety of greens and fresh twigs and leaf buds daily.

Since white-eared conures are birds that should definitely be kept outside (even during the winter, when they must have access to a draft-free and frost-free shelter), they are less suitable for keeping indoors and are truly at their best when kept in a roomy aviary. They withstand cold temperatures and even dampness quite well, though of course we should never unnecessarily subject them to these discomforts. In their native land they do quite a lot of damage; cornfields are completely picked clean (I have witnessed this myself) and they are a true plague! As a consequence, they are often shot down, which may seem cruel in our eyes, but from the farmer's point of view it's a bitter necessity.

The birds live together in groups that number 20-26. A couple kept in a roomy cage will do quite well (place the cage outside as much as possible), but when kept in a roomy aviary without other birds they will breed regularly. When kept indoors they can learn to say a few words, though they will never become great debaters!

Here is a good tip with regard to determining the sex: males can generally be identified by a broader head, and they are also usually more aggressive than females. I personally consider this bird the most beautiful species of the genus. There are still four other subspecies: *Pyrrhura leucotis griseipectus* (eastern Brazil); *Pyrrhura leucotis pfrimeri* (Goyaz); *Pyrrhura leucotis emma* (from the coastal regions of Venezuela to the border of Brazil and up to the Caribbean); and *Pyrrhura leucotis auricularis* (north-eastern Venezuela).

There are a few other species belonging to *Pyrrhura* which I would like to call the blue-winged pyrrhuras. The most obvious characteristics of the first one I wish to describe, namely *Pyrrhura picta picta,* is the blue in the wings, the red on the curve of the wing, the black on the head and in the neck, the blue on the forehead, and the green in the upper part of the breast. The throat is brown, the upper cheeks have a brown hue while the lower cheek area is blue, and the area around the ear is grayish. The scalloped marking on the breast is reddish to yellowish brown. The underside reveals some tinges of red, and the tail is also reddish brown underneath.

186

There are four other closely related species and species that are sometimes offered for sale, but unfortunately are often confused with one another by both the fancier and the bird dealer because they do not know or cannot see their differences. No doubt the following notations may be of some use.

Firstly there is the painted conure (*Pyrrhura picta amazonum*), which hails from the valley of the Lower Amazon. This bird is regularly offered for sale and is known as Lucian's conure. It differs from the previous birds because of a salmon-pink color on the forehead and around its dark eyes. The cheeks have a vague blue color and are bordered by brownish yellow bands. The feathers of its underside reveal a little chestnut coloring.

Hoffman's conure (*Pyrrhura hoffmanni gaudens*), from the Amazon region, has bright red cheeks and yellow colors on an otherwise bright green head. There is no red on the underparts of this bird's body, but there is some yellow in the wings; the cere is a light horn color. Obviously the characteristic red in the under tail-coverts is present in this bird also. The bird has a very slender build. Another subspecies is *Pyrrhura hoffmanni hoffmanni*, which is even brighter in colors and markings.

The red-eared conure (*Pyrrhura hoematotis*) is smaller than the previous bird and hails from northern Venezuela. This species has a bronzy face with black and a few red and chestnut feathers in the area around the ears and cheeks. The light beak is horn-colored. The flanks are red and there is some blue in the wings. The inside of the wings are green with a bluish glow. The large primaries are gray-black.

Even less well known as aviary birds are the following:

Blaze-winged conure (*Pyrrhura devillei*) - Eastern Bolivia and southern Matto Grosso area.

Crimson-bellied conure (*Pyrrhura rhodogaster*) - rarely seen offered for sale.

Green-cheeked conure (*Pyrrhura molinae*) - has five sub-species: *phoenicura,* from the west-central Matto Grasso region; *molinae* from easter Bolivia; *australis* from southern Bolivia and Argentina; *sordida* from southern Matto Grosso (Brazil) and eastern Bolivia and Argentina; *restricta* from Palmarito, Chiquitos (Brazil).

Santa Marta conure (*Pyrrhura viridicata*) - from the Santa

The Australian king parrot, *Alisterus scapularis,* is not as active or noisy as most other parrots, and it makes an excellent aviary bird.

Crimson rosella, *Platycercus elegans;* this bird can be kept in an outdoor aviary year-round if a well covered shelter is provided.

Marta Mountains in Colombia.

Fiery-shouldered conure (*Pyrrhura egregia*) - from Guyana, with two subspecies: *egregia* and *obscura*.

Maroon-tailed conure (*Pyrrhura melanura*) - has five subspecies: *melanura, souancei, pacifica, berlepschi,* and *chapmani.*

Black-capped conure (*Pyrrhura rupicola*) - with two subspecies: *rupicola* and *sandiae.*

White-necked conure (*Pyrrhura albipectus*).

Brown-breasted conure (*Pyrrhura calliptera*).

Rose-crowned conure (*Pyrrhura rhodocephala*).

Yellow-sided conure (*Pyrrhura hypoxantha*) - from the western Matto Grasso region.

Further studies will be necessary before we can definitely determine the actual regions these birds inhabit and their status.

GENUS *BOLBORHYNCHUS*

Birds belonging to this genus have long, pointed wings and a long, fancy tail.

Barred Parrakeet (*Bolborhynchus lineola lineola*)

Distribution: Central America from Mexico to Panama.

Male: Primarily green, with black shell-shaped markings on the head, neck, back, rump, and along the wings. The feathers of the wings are bordered with black. Yellow-brown eyes, gray-yellow beak, and gray-black feet.

Female: Somewhat smaller than the male, but has the same black markings, although they are smaller and less sharply defined.

Offspring: Although they soon resemble the adult birds after losing their nest down, they have a vague buffy look which gives their plumage a duller appearance. The beak and feet, on the other hand, are bright in color, which makes them readily distinguishable from their parents.

Particulars: This bird is a typical mountain inhabitant and is not really in his element until he is at an elevation of some 2000 meters (6500 feet) above sea level. This species has a noteworthy reaction when being intensively hunted: they "squat" in the event of danger, a phenomenon that also occurs with some waterfowl species. When the danger draws too near the birds fly upward, screaming loudly, and fall victim to the murderous guns of their pursuers if they do not quickly find refuge in the thorny underbrush. In captivity, however, these much-hunted birds will become tame very quickly and leave all signs of timidity behind. They have a strong constitution and are affectionate toward their keeper. Both in an aviary and a roomy cage they will breed well and regularly. In the wild they make their nests in tree hollows (for nest box requirements see the white-eared conure). The young leave the nest in June but will still be fed by the male for some time. The female usually lays two eggs per clutch; these measure 20x18 mm.

Their song, in contrast to that of many parrakeets and parrots, is not at all unpleasant. If we have a lot of patience, we can also teach them to say a few words. They do quite well in a community aviary and are basically very tolerant birds. When they become excited they show their emotions by fanning their tails. They live on oats, panicum, and canary seeds, as well as fresh twigs, particularly from pear and apple trees. They are also particularly fond of various types of fruit and berries. This species lives mainly on the ground, where they seek small insects. In the aviary too, one can observe them constantly looking for insects, which is why it is a good idea to deeply rake the ground for them a few times each week. They also spend some time in the trees, where they climb from branch to branch with head stretched out and held low, much like a cat stalking its prey.

Since the color differences between the sexes are not always clear, one may conduct the pelvic bone test often used with lovebirds: if the pelvic bones are closed or almost closed, we are dealing with a male; if we can feel a narrow opening with our thumb, we are holding a female.

Ornithologists recognize two more subspecies. I feel, however, that *Bolborhynchus lineola maculatus* from the east of Peru is synonymous with *Bolborhynchus lineola tigrinus,* which can be found from the Andes to Colombia. Two other species, *Bolborhynchus ferrugineifrons* (rufous-fronted parrakeet) and *Bolbor-*

The Yellow-fronted parrakeet, *Cyanoramphus auriceps,* from New Zealand.

The nanday conure, *Nandayus nenday,* also known as the black-headed conure, cheerfully emits a shrill chatter when perching.

194

4

1. Eastern rosella. 2. A pair of western rosellas, male right, female left. 3. Red-winged parrot. 4. Cockatiels, albino and pied. 5. Bourke's parrots.

5

195

1

1. The scarlet-chested parrot, *Neophema splendida,* is one of the most expensive parrots—but rightfully so, as they are one of the most beautiful. 2. A red mutation of the scarlet-chested parrot. 3. Male red mutation of the scarlet-chested parrot.

2

3

hynchus orbygnesius (Andean parrakeet), both of which inhabit the Andes regions to Peru, are never to my knowledge offered for sale on the market, so that I think my simply mentioning them by name is sufficient.

GENUS *BROTOGERIS*

These are charming birds, both in the wild and in an aviary or cage. They have long, pointed wings that cover about three-quarters of their tail; the tail itself is shaped like a wedge. There are seven species that live from southern Mexico to central South America. When they are on a hunt they become quite rash, particularly when they are together in a group and land, for example, in a corn field.

During the breeding season they are extremely difficult toward other birds in the aviary and certainly toward their own species. Outside the breeding season, however, they do not pose any danger to breeding exotic birds and will, in general, do nothing to bother them. Observations reveal they simply do not come into the immediate vicinity of the busy tropical birds. A bird alone or with a mate should have a cage that measures at least 70-80 cm long, 60 cm deep and 80 cm high (28-32x24x32 inches).

Their menu should consist of cherries, apples, pears, bananas, pineapples (in pieces), soaked raisins and currants, corn, rice, oats, fresh buds, various grasses, sometimes hemp, and small earth beetles (no dangerous sorts of course, and only from earth that has not been treated with chemical fertilizers).

These birds often have their wings clipped before they are shipped from their native country. Quite frequently clipped birds still arrive on the market, and these will need to be housed separately for some time and given extra nutrition in the form of rice and willow-bark. Only when our bird has calmed down properly (initially he will be very timid and restless and as a consequence clamber around his cage constantly) and his wings have grown back to their proper length should he be allowed into the aviary. In spite of their deafening calls, these primarily green birds are quite popular among bird fanciers; their slender build makes one think more of a parrot than a parrakeet.

Orange-chinned Parrakeet (*Brotogeris jugularis*)

Distribution: Southern Mexico to Colombia.

Male and Female: Green; clear yellow patch on throat. Wing-coverts greenish brown; balance bluish green. Primaries dark blue. Inside of wings are bright yellow except for a few large greenish blue feathers. Brown eyes, grayish black beak; dark, flesh-colored feet.

Length: 18-20 cm (7 1/5-8 inches); wings 10-12 cm (4-4 4/5 inches).

Offspring: The young resemble the adult birds once they have lost their bleak grayish nest down, although the lovely shine of the adults is not yet present, giving the colors a duller appearance.

Particulars: In the wild this species lives together in small troops (10-18 birds) in the woods (though they will go up to approximately 1000 meters (3300 feet) above sea level in the mountains), where they look for fruit, soft leaf buds, twigs, and berries. The young are also raised, in large part, on soft fruit. They are fond of insects.

Because of their pleasant nature they make excellent aviary birds that will soon be on good terms with their aviary-mates. They cannot tolerate draft and wind very well, and during the winter months should be placed in a large cage in a room or attic where the temperature will not go as low as the freezing point. Providing this room with some heat (such as thermostatically controlled electric heaters) can only do them good. During the breeding season the female lays two or three eggs; quite often a pair will raise as many as two or even three broods per year!

In addition to the regular menu, it is advisable to provide them with corn, rice, fruit (see also the general notes for this genus), fresh twigs and leaf buds and soaked stale white bread; during the breeding period these are absolutely essential.

These colorful birds are quite regularly offered for sale in pet shops. Remember that recently imported birds require some careful conditioning and should be placed in a warm area, preferably in a large cage, so that their movements will not be hindered. In this way they will gradually become accustomed to our particular local climate. We must not forget to offer them various types of fruit and could actually consider fruit as their main fare, particularly for recently imported specimens. The bottom of the

A male turquoise parrot, differing from the female by having a slightly more brilliant overall color, more blue on the face and markings of deep red on the wings.

A female turquoise parrot, *Neophema pulchella.* This bird is called a "bird of the twilight," as it chooses that time of the day to become most active.

cage should be covered with brown paper or wood shavings (not newspapers or printed circulars); replacing these regularly is, of course, no luxury! These birds need to have a nesting box available to them 40 x 30 x 40 cm (16 x 12 x 16 inches), entrance 8 cm (3 1/5 inches) in diameter, because they also use this as sleeping quarters.

During the first weeks after their arrival, we may find that they are still somewhat suspicious of us, but after a while they will become very tame, even finger-tame, particularly if we treat them in a friendly manner and guarantee them good care.

Some ornithologists recognize four subspecies, namely: *Brotogeris jugularis cyanoptera* (branches of the Amazon); *Brotogeris jugularis jugularis* (southwestern Mexico to northern Colombia); *Brotogeris jugularis exsul* (northern Venezuela); and *Brotogeris jugularis apurensis* (central western Venezuela). Unfortunately, due to the minute differences between them merchants often confuse them, selling one for the other, but even ornithologists have trouble in telling them apart. Forshaw regards *cyanoptera* or the cobalt-winged parrakeet (with 3 subspecies) as a full species.

Plain Parrakeet (*Brotogeris tirica*)

Distribution: Eastern Brazil.

Male and Female: Green with blue primaries and flanks. The tail also has some blue feathers. Brown eyes, pinkish red beak, and brownish gray feet. Due to their slender build and coloring, one is reminded of the previous species.

Length: 25-26 cm (10-10 4/5 inches); wings 8-12 cm (3 1/5-4 4/5 inches); tail 10-15 cm (2-3 inches).

Particulars: Although seldom imported, these birds are favorites with experienced fanciers, particularly in their land of origin. They live in large troops, sometimes in the company of different birds such as the jandaya conure, with which, strangely enough, they never mate. They can cause quite some damage to corn fields as well as to fruit orchards and young trees. The female lays two to four eggs (19x15 mm). The young birds leave the nest in July to early August, but will still be fed by their parents for some time to come.

Tui Parrakeet (*Brotogeris sanctithomae santithomae*)

Distribution: Western Brazil, Peru, Lower Amazon, and Ecuador.

Male and Female: Light green. Primaries blue/gray/green. Bright yellow crown and neck. Eyes are bordered with light green. Clearly defined yellow stripe by eye in male only. Some yellow can be seen shining through the feathers of the breast and along the wings. Brown eyes, grayish yellow to grayish red beak (the beak is smaller in the female, which is another excellent way to determine the sex). The feet are light gray to grayish black.

Length: 17-18½ cm (6 4/5-7 3/5 inches); wings 10-10½ cm (4 inches); tail 5-6 cm (2-2 2/5 inches).

Particulars: This forest inhabitant is a very pleasant bird towards both its fellow species and finches, which makes it a very suitable candidate for a community aviary. Feeding particulars coincide with those listed under the genus.

The female lays four to five eggs (23x17 mm) in a nest that is built by a joint effort of both male and female. In the wild the nest is usually built about 5 meters (16 feet) from the ground, well hidden between branches and leaves. Noteworthy is the fact that, according to the famous Australian researcher and ornithologist Barrett, these birds sometimes make their nest in termite hills, which I was personally able to witness in 1969-1970 in Peru. It is a pity, actually, that this bird is seldom seen on the market; I would think that this bird should be much better known among fanciers. Whenever they are offered for sale, and of course this does happen once in a while, they are not even all that expensive, so that any bird enthusiast could be able to procure a pair.

As already mentioned, these are very friendly birds and quite suitable for living together with different species in a large aviary that has a lot of shrubbery. We must keep in mind, however, that the other aviary mates must not belong to the same species (and related species are generally not accepted as well as totally unrelated species either) because we may then, although not necessarily, run into a situation where little quarrels arise among them and, although they may not be of a serious nature, would still disturb the total peace that should reign to promote success during the breeding season. Recently imported specimens must, of course, be acclimated with care.

1

2

3

1. The turquoise parrot, *Neophema pulchella,* from scattered areas of Australia is so uncommon that until recently it was thought to be extinct. 2. Elegant parrot, *Neophema elegans* (foreground) and red-rump, *Psephotus haematonotus* (on wire mesh). 3. Purple-crowned lorikeet, *Glossopsitta porphyrocephala.* This is the only lorikeet known to inhabit western Australia. Its coloring provides good camouflage in the foliage where it feeds, but its noisy chatter always reveals its whereabouts.

205

Once they have become accustomed to both food and aviary, they will become tame and be prepared to breed quite quickly. A roomy beechwood nesting box would be ideal; we must be sure though, that the entrance hole is situated in a location that will allow the bird sitting on the eggs to be able to look outside. The female tends to be a little jumpy, and she likes to be able to see what is going on around her.

Golden-winged Parrakeet (*Brotogeris chrysopterus tuipara*)

Distribution: Lower Amazon.

Male and female: Primarily green, lighter underneath. Bluish black shine on head. Orange stripe runs across forehead; orange-yellow spot on chin. Some yellow feathers in the wings and tail. The primaries are a shiny bluish black, ending in dark green. The eyes are brown (encircled with a bare greenish blue eye-ring). The beak is light gray and the feet are pinkish red.

Length: 20 cm (8 inches); wings 11½-12½ cm (4 3/5-5 inches); tail 6-8 cm (2 2/5-3 1/5 inches).

Particulars: Fortunately we are seeing more and more of these beautiful birds in the trade in recent years. They are selling well in spite of their fairly high prices, and their popularity is understandable when we consider their rich, colorful beauty and the fact that they can be easily tamed. I feel they are not quite as suitable for keeping indoors, due to their not so pleasant song, but this does not seem to hinder the great many people that keep them in their homes. They are, in any event, excellent in an aviary. They are generally tolerant of other exotic birds that might share the aviary with them, such as finches, doves, and quail. In order to achieve successful breeding results, we should house them in an aviary of generous dimensions. Their aviary should be equipped with extra branches for climbing, since climbing is something they love to do (although they are not all that good at it!). For breeding data you are referred to the details given about the tui parrakeet.

Canary-winged Parrakeet (*Brotogeris versicolorus chiriri*)

Distribution: Bolivia, eastern and central Brazil, eastern Peru.

Male and Female: Primarily green, darker on breast and belly.

Outermost wing-feather edges, epaulet, and primaries are bright yellow. Underside of tail is blue. Dark brown eyes; light, horn-colored beak; and pinkish-red feet. Sometimes there is some blue in the wings. The coloring of the offspring is generally a little duller, particularly the blue and yellow hues.

Length: 23-25 cm (9 1/5-10 inches); wings about 12 cm (4 4/5 inches); tail 13 cm (5 1/5 inches).

Particulars: This is a well known species due to its beautiful coloring and slender build. It also possesses a pleasant nature and, like some of the other *Brotogeris* species, sometimes builds its nest in termite hills, though more often in trees as we had the opportunity to see during a study trip in 1969-70. The female lays four to six eggs (22-23 x 18-19 mm).

The canary-winged parrakeet lives in small flocks close to forests and also to towns. Their popularity has increased quite a bit during the last fifteen years because their care is relatively simple and they are also inexpensive. I should remind you again to procure an agreement from the seller that will allow you to exchange one of the birds should your couple not form a true pair. Once we are in possession of a true pair, we can be assured that sooner or later they will start with the business of building a nest. One of the reasons they breed so well is their friendly and peaceful nature. Providing they receive good and proper care, they can become finger-tame in just a few weeks, and from such birds good breeding results are the norm. It is a pity that they have a fairly loud, somewhat raucous call, which they may give voice to if they are excited, or even content, though I imagine this would not be of any concern if they are kept in an outside aviary. My birds in Australia, however, were kept indoors and were possessed of a great deal of charm. They even spoke a few words in both English and Dutch, and my wife had even taught them Shakespeare's eternal words in *Hamlet* "To be or not to be." This little phrase could sound incredibly funny when uttered in certain situations. The beechwood nesting boxes should be equipped with a layer of moist peat moss about 4 cm (1½ ") thick. In order to assure the best possible breeding results, the nesting boxes should be hung outside during the winter months, providing they have access to a draft-and rain-free night shelter.

In the southern regions of Bolivia lives another subspecies,

1. Golden-shouldered parrakeet, *Psephotus c. chrysopterygius.* This beautiful bird is very rare and is quickly approaching extinction. 2. Hooded parrakeet, *P. c. dissimilis.* 3. Golden shouldered parrakeet, *Psephotus c. chrysopterygius.*

scientifically known as the *Brotogeris versicolorus behni*, that is very similar to the bird described above. Another subspecies is *Brotogeris versicolorus versicolorus*, seldom seen in the trade. This bird differs from its relatives by the stripe in the wings that is whitish but has a yellowish shine. This subspecies lives in the valley of the Amazon and requires the same care as the previous types.

Grey-cheeked Parrakeet (*Brotogeris pyrrhopterus*)

Distribution: Northwestern Peru and western Ecuador.

Male and female: Deep blue-green head; back and rump are green. Grayish forehead, cheeks, and upper breast. Wing borders and primaries deep blue. Feathers of the wings are mostly bordered in yellow. Bright orange on inside of wings. . .justice is really done to this beauty when the bird is in flight. Brownish black eyes; beak and feet pinkish red.

Length: 21 cm (8 2/5 inches); wings 10-12 cm (4-4 4/5 inches); tail 6-8 cm (2 2/5-3 1/5 inches).

Particulars: In its native country this species is often kept as a cage bird. They are also hunted extensively because of the damage they do to the banana plantations. In the aviary we should regularly offer them small pieces of banana, which these pleasant, lively birds will consider a real treat.

Grey-cheeked parrakeets build their nest, according to the ornithologist Barrett, in termite mounds, but also use the hollows of trees. They furnish their nest with a layer of moist moss on which they lay four to six eggs (20-22 x 16-18 mm). Only the female will hatch them; the male guards the nest from a nearby post.

A strange phenomenon with this species is that they gather in trees at certain set times, just as, for example, the starlings will do when the fall draws near. Sometimes the trees near a town are full of them, especially around early evening. At such a time the air is filled with their constant chattering. With a little patience these birds can be taught to cry, laugh, and speak. It is a pity, however, that they are not all that well known. If we search long enough we are sure to find some offered for sale, but the prices are quite high.

If we want them to breed, we should supply them with a large nesting box 35x50 cm (14x20 inches); the entrance opening should have an 8 cm (3 1/5 inches) diameter. The bottom is covered with a thick layer of moss or peatmoss at least 6 to 8 cm (2 2/5-3 1/5 inches) and hung as high as possible, facing north. It is wise not to have any fellow species in the aviary during the breeding season. Finches, doves, and quail will not cause any problems; unless your collection includes a troublemaker among them, the parrakeets will not bother them! These birds may be kept outdoors during the winter months, as long as they have a draft- and rain-free night shelter available to them; this is a requirement, of course, that really applies to all birds.

Brotogeris cyanoptera gustavi lives in eastern Peru. It is a very rare bird in the wild and is totally unknown as an aviary bird.

GENUS *ARATINGA*

Birds that have been designated by ornithologists as belonging to the genus *Aratinga* fall under the classification of conures, which is why until recently "conure" was part of their scientific name. The *Aratinga* species come in many different plumages, and even their size and origin are not common denominators. They all come from the New World, from Mexico south to most parts of South America, and they generally have a clearly defined eye-ring. Some species have a fairly broad periophthalmic region. The mandibles, which are never red, are sturdy and thick in build. Unlike the previous genus, the upper and lower mandibles are not so strong when clamped shut. The tail has the shape of a wedge and has smaller dimensions than the long and pointed wings. The last four feathers of the wings are noticeably narrow in shape. Most of the species are primarily green in color and have a slender build and a large head and beak. They live in either jungles or mountains (up to the tree line) or in the 'wide open spaces'. . .but always together in small troops. Some species even stay together in troops during the breeding season.

Their menu should consist of grass seeds, hemp, oats, fruit, fresh buds, boiled or soaked seeds, corn, soaked white bread, live foods (mealworms, white worms, ant-eggs, etc.), nuts, berries, etc. From their food preferences the reader can surmise that they are

1. Red-winged parrot, *Aprosmictus e. erythropterus.* This magnificent bird is an avicultural favorite. It is very fond of bathing and should be encouraged but well protected from chills. 2. Red-winged parrot male. 3. Another view of a red-winged parrot female.

3

quite damaging to many agricultural efforts and as a result are hunted virtually the year-round.

They build their nests in hollows of trees ("nest" in this case being a euphemism), so we should supply them with roomy nesting boxes in the aviary. Some species even build their nests in rock crevices. Practically all of the species are partly migratory. Those birds are not suitable for keeping in a community type aviary; they will peck at fellow species and any other species which comes too close to them, and their loud constant screeching would, no doubt, be very disturbing to any birds that are breeding, including those in the immediate vicinity but not in the same aviary. This screeching also makes them poor candidates for keeping inside, though I have seen several kept as pets in South America, sitting on their perches and talking a great deal. They can be tamed quite quickly and can be very affectionate as well. When they are tame their screeching is reduced considerably (and no doubt some birds are just worse "screechers" than others anyway), but it is still my opinion that they are at their best when kept in a large aviary. Initially they will probably have some difficulty in adjusting to aviary life, but if we leave them alone for the first few weeks, things will probably fall into place well enough. If we wish to keep them on a perch, this would need to be at least 75 cm (30 inches) long and about 1 meter (3 feet) for the larger species. Of the many species belonging to this genus, we will discuss only the more important ones.

Peach-Fronted Conure (*Aratinga aurea aurea*)

Distribution: Brazil

Male and female: Yellow-orange crown, bordered with blue. Eyes bordered with an orange band. Dark green neck and rump, the balance of the bird primarily light green with a yellowish green belly. Blue shades can be seen shining through in the wing feathers. Insides of the wings are light green to yellowish green. Eyes orange to brown, beak and feet grayish black.

Length: 28-29 cm (11 1/5-11 3/5 inches); wings 14-15 cm (5 3/5-6 inches); tail 13-14 cm (5 1/5-5 3/5 inches).

Particulars: The female lays two eggs (28-29 x 21-22 mm). Both the male and female sit on the eggs, which take about four weeks before they are hatched. The nesting box should have the following dimensions: 35 cm long and 22-25 cm wide (14 x 9-10 inches); the entrance opening should have a diameter of 8 cm (3 1/5 inches). When they are provided with such a nesting box, there is every likelihood that they will breed a second time.

The young resemble the parents, although the colors are less sharp. When they leave the nest at about 50 days, it is advisable to remove fellow species from the aviary, because the male will very actively defend his young. This attitude can be observed in a somewhat less fiery manner during prior stages of the breeding cycle as well. In captivity these birds become rapidly attached to their keeper; in fact, with a little patience they can be taught to speak a few words and even simple sentences. A breeder told me that young independent birds can even be taught to whistle a simple tune!

More and more of these birds are being offered on the market, and their prices are quite reasonable. Once they have become acclimated, they can remain outside during the winter months, providing, again, they have access to a draft- and rain-free night shelter.

Another subspecies, *Aratinga aurea major,* lives in the vicinity of the Paraguay River in Paraguay and is so similar to the peach-fronted conure that they are constantly confusing breeders and fanciers alike being sold one for the other as a consequence.

Brown-throated Conure (*Aratinga pertinax pertinax*)

Distribution: Curacao and St. Thomas.

Male and female: Primarily green, with bright yellow forehead, cheeks, and chin. Bluish black crown. Throat grayish brown, slowly changing to orange-yellow toward the belly. Clearly visible bluish black spot on the tail formed by four tail feathers attached at one point. Brown eyes, blackish gray beak and white cere; feet are gray-black to brown.

Length: 25-26 cm (12-12 2/5 inches); wings 12-14 cm (4 4/5-5 3/5 inches); tail 9-12 cm (3 3/5-4 4/5 inches).

Particulars: The female is generally a little smaller in build 23-25 cm (9 1/5-10 inches) and her coloring is also a little duller

1. A pair of cockatiels, *Nymphicus hollandicus.* The sex can be determined only by careful examination of the flight feathers. 2. Clipping the wing of a cockatiel, a task for the experienced only. 3. A wild male cockatiel resting on a branch.

than the male's. Nevertheless, picking out a true pair can pose a few problems. They are very peace-loving birds and get along with each other very well; this, in itself, does not simplify the matter of determining the sex of the bird. You may, for example, end up with two males or two females, even though the two birds act as if they are a pair. So if you wish to buy a pair, the advice of your local dealer should come in handy. These birds are offered for sale regularly, so a possible exchange should not cause any difficulties.

Their screeching is far from pleasant, being raucous and sharp, particularly when they have not yet become accustomed to the aviary and their new surroundings. After a few weeks they generally become a lot more peaceful and may even take food out of your hand. Their nutritional requirements are as follows: sunflower seeds, corn (preferably on the cob), hemp, soaked stale white bread, nuts, berries, hard-boiled eggs, and definitely fresh twigs and buds (willow, hazel, etc.).

This species will not breed very easily in captivity. A friend of mine, however, had a pair of brown-throated conures that built a nest in a nesting box which measured 30 x 30 cm (12 x 12 inches), entrance opening diameter of 8 cm (3 1/5 inches). The female laid two eggs, which were subsequently hatched and the babies reared beautifully. The same couple reared two offspring the year before. Only the female sat on the eggs, while the male constantly brought food to her. In the wild this species prefers to make their nests in termite hills.

The brown-throated conures can usually be housed in a community aviary. Their movements through the branches are not that fast, so that other birds should have no difficulty in getting away from them should their sturdy beaks threaten to come too close. There are cases where the conures constantly peck at their aviary mates, which should certainly disqualify them from community living. Tame birds are most unlikely to pose any such problems.

There are a few other subspecies I would like to mention, for instance *Aratinga pertinax ocularis* from Panama, which has brown cheeks and throat. This is a charming bird that will become a great little friend if given good care and treated with a friendly attitude. Since its colors are not so striking, there is not as much demand for this bird as I feel it deserves. Another subspecies is *Aratinga pertinax aeruginosa,* which has a grayish white beak and less brown in the cheeks. This bird also is rarely made available on the market. On Margarita Island and the Paria Peninsula of Venezuela there is yet another brown-throated subspecies, *Aratinga pertinax margaritensis.* Along the coast of Venezuela is where *Aratinga pertinax tortugensis* makes its home, especially on Tortuga Island.

Better known and therefore more comprehensively covered is the following subspecies:

Aratinga pertinax chrysophrys

Distribution: Guyana, Cayenne, and Surinam.

Male and female: Primarily green with yellow cheeks and chin. Some blue-black on the crown. Grayish throat, orange-yellow belly. The tail has a bluish black point. Brown eyes, grayish black beak with white cere, and grayish black to brown feet. I would like to point out that the colorings of the above mentioned subspecies are all quite similar. This particular subspecies differs from the others because of its orange flanks and the bare blue area around the eyes.

Length: 25-26 cm (10-10 2/5 inches); wings 13 cm (5 1/5 inches); tail 11 cm (4 2/5 inches).

Particulars: This subspecies has enjoyed increasing popularity over the last few years. Since determining their sex is quite difficult, we will need to make an agreement with the seller allowing us to exchange one of our birds should our "pair" not be a true pair.

I have learned from experience that these birds are ambitious breeders, providing they have a good nesting box 30 x 25 cm (12 x 10 inches); entrance hole 8 cm in diameter (3 1/5 inches) hung high up in the aviary. Several authors advised us to hang the box facing north, but more recent works do not mention this. Personally, I have had three consecutive successes with a couple that was housed in an aviary measuring 2 x 2 x 2½ meters (6 x 6 x 7½ feet) and where the nesting box was not able to face north because of technical reasons; this should put an interesting slant on the theory of having the box face north. From these experiences I have concluded that it does not make much difference in which direction the nesting box opening faces. While in Florida I had four

A 48 day old pale-headed Rosella, *Platycercus adscitus.*

The eastern rosella, *Platycercus eximius,* is a common inhabitant of parks and gardens in the cities of south-eastern Australia where it occurs.

1. Port Lincoln parrot. 2 and 3. Eastern rosellas. A roomy aviary is well suited to this bird. 4. Red-rumped parrakeet. 5. Red-rumped parakeets are ideal foster parents for all grass parrakeets. These parrakeets may be kept in a large aviary with other birds, but not with their own kind. Their origin is southern and southeastern Australia. 6. Red-rumped and Bourke's parrots showing suitable nestbox for both species.

4

5

6

The golden-mantled rosella, *Platycercus eximius cecilae,* has been so often crossed with the eastern rosella, *Platycercus eximius,* that a purebred golden-mantled is difficult to find.

Pale-headed rosella, *Platycercus a. adscitus,* from northeastern Australia. Young birds of this species remain with their parents to form small family parties.

couples that bred well each year, and none of their boxes faced north either. I do not mean to imply that I advise against hanging the boxes so that they face north; I just do not see much sense to it.

Experience has also taught me that *chrysophrys* are peace-loving birds which will seldom fight and can live very well with three or four other parrakeet couples (not too small, however) in one aviary. Naturally, it goes without saying that to ensure good breeding results a separate aviary for each couple is the most likely road to success. We should also make sure that our birds are not disturbed during the breeding season. Dogs and cats should be kept out of the way. The bottom of the nesting box should be covered with a firmly packed down layer of moss or peatmoss which we must thoroughly moisten, because only then will we have a good chance of having the eggs hatch. If we purchase (or make) nesting boxes with a double bottom, we can repeatedly moisten the moss so that there will always be enough humidity.

The female lays two to four eggs (28 x 21 mm) that take about four weeks to hatch. In the wild the male and female take turns in sitting on the eggs. In captivity it is mostly the female that hatches them, although the male, as a rule, joins her in the box at night. I am not sure if he actually sits on the eggs then or not, but on a few occasions I have seen that the female keeps the eggs underneath her. The young leave the nest when they are 40-50 days old, though they will still receive some care from their parents. I have often seen the male take food to the female during the breeding period, but I would not venture to say that this is the rule.

These birds can stay outside during the winter. Although I may have brought the following fact to your attention previously, I would like to emphasize its importance once more, especially because *chrysophrys* are so sensitive in their feet . . . we will need to be ever watchful for frozen feet during the winter with all parrakeet varieties. We should make it a rule to check each night to be sure that they are all in the night shelter. When we build our aviary in such a manner that the roof of the night shelter is higher than the flight, the birds will just naturally go to sleep in the shelter. If we have a door that divides shelter and flight and close this at night after checking on our birds, this would be ideal, since chances of draft and frost will be minimized this way as well. We could also create a better temperature for our birds with a thermostatically controlled electric heater or the like, though we must be sure not to make the temperature too warm, since they may then catch cold during the day. An ounce of prevention is better than a pound of cure, and this certainly applies here; in other words, if we have any space available indoors, it is advisable to move our birds inside for the winter. We will then not need to worry about providing heat either.

Finally, I would like to point out that although these birds can be kept together with other parrakeet and parrot varieties, and even an occasional quail, we should never house more than one couple together in a community aviary because they will fight with their own species. It would not be the first time that one or more casualties resulted from these fights.

A subspecies very similar to *chrysophrys* is *Aratinga pertinax arubensis* from Aruba. Both subspecies are constantly being confused on the market place. Another subspecies is *Aratinga pertinax xanthogenia*, which hails from Bonaire.

Red-Fronted Conure (*Aratinga wagleri frontata*)

Distribution: Ecuador and western Peru.

Male and female: Red forehead, crown, collar, bend of wing, flanks, and outer edge of wings. Recently imported birds show blackish purple markings on the wings that become paler with birds in captivity. The rest of the body is green. Yellow-brown eyes and grayish white beak; brown feet.

Length: 37-39 cm (14 4/5-15 3/5 inches); wings 18 cm (7 1/5 inches). The female is a few centimeters smaller, and the red on her wings is often duller. In general, there is little difference between the sexes.

Particulars: These gorgeous, quickly tamed birds are regularly available on the market for fairly reasonable prices. Beginning bird fanciers/breeders could well choose this species to start with, because their care is relatively simple. This bird is also very suitable for keeping indoors in a cage and is certainly one of the best talkers. My wife had a red-fronted conure during her youth who could quote a few lines (if not all that clearly of course) of Keats' work, *Endymion:* "A thing of beauty is a joy forever; Its loveliness increases; it will never pass into nothingness." This

Eastern rosella, *Platycercus eximius,* a popular bird found in southeastern Australia and Tasmania; the male has more red on the upper chest.

Pale-headed rosella, *Platycercus adscitus,* also known as the blue rosella, from the northeastern regions of Australia. This bird is not a favorite of collectors.

bird attracted quite some interest in Tampa and was so tame that she could accompany my wife on her shoulder on the way to college and remain in the trees by the school until my wife returned to pick her up again.

As far as I know, no breeding results have been achieved in captivity, but there is no reason why this could not be changed if we have a couple accommodated in a roomy aviary.

The subspecies *Aratinga wagleri wagleri,* from Colombia and the northern coastal region of western Venezuela, is primarily green with a red forehead. The beak is a light horn color. *Aratinga wagleri transilis* comes from the northeastern region of Venezuela, and here again there are only small differences between these subspecies. As far as I was able to determine, aviculturists do not even recognize them as different, which ornithologically speaking, of course, is very unfortunate. The subspecies *Aratinga wagleri minor* hails from north-central Peru and differs from *Aratinga wagleri frontata* because of its small build.

Cactus Conure (*Aratinga cactorum cactorum*)

Distribution: Brazil.

Male and female: Green neck, back, and rump. Brown-white forehead; bluish white crown. Grayish brown cheeks; light brown throat. Very obvious yellow stripe over the eye. Golden yellow breast, becoming darker toward the belly. Long pointed wings that are green with blue markings. The tail is also green with bluish green borders. Eyes yellow to brown; brownish gray beak and flesh-colored feet. Although it is not easy to determine the sex, a knowledgeable fancier will not have that much trouble, especially if he can compare the birds sitting next to each other. The female's coloring is less sharp. Once again, however, this only becomes clear when we can compare the birds together.

Length: 25 cm (10 inches); wings 12-14 cm (4 4/5-5 3/5 inches); tail 12-13 cm (4 4/5-5 1/5 inches).

Particulars: These somewhat monotonously colored birds live in the wild in small groups on the plains, in the thick underbrush, the high trees, or in high grass and weeds. They are quite suitable for either a roomy cage or an aviary, though I must add that, to my knowledge, no breeding results have as yet been achieved in captivity, although a few of the top aviculturists have attempted it. This is why they are often kept as just decorative pets in either aviary or cage, though to do them justice we must add that they learn to speak quite readily and are very affectionate as well. They make good cage birds, too, because their voices are not all that bothersome. If we frequently offer our pet a few pieces of sweet apple, a variety of greens, parrakeet seed, and such, I am convinced you will enjoy a great deal of pleasure from your bird. I believe this is one of the most affectionate pets we can have in our home. Beginners in this field would do well to choose the cactus conure.

It may be interesting to know that in the wild this species lives primarily on cactus seeds—hence its name— as well as fruit and berries. If you wish to give them an extra treat, we advise half a slice of stale white bread soaked in natural honey and milk.

Another subspecies, *Aratinga cactorum caixana,* is a native of eastern Brazil and hardly differs from *cactorum cactorum.*

White-eyed Conure (*Aratinga leucophthalmus leucophthalmus*)

Distribution: Most of tropical South America, including the Guianas, Colombia, Bolivia, and Brazil.

Male and female: Primarily green, some have red on the head. The underside of the wings is yellow, small wing-coverts bright red; the wing itself is edged in red. Flesh-colored beak and a grayish black to pink feet. Grayish white naked periophthalmic ring; iris orange to brown.

Length: 33-35 cm (13 1/5-14 inches); wings 15-18 cm (6-7 1/5 inches); tail 11-17 cm (4 2/5-6 4/5 inches).

Particulars: These very lively birds live together in small groups on the savannahs or in the forest. In the wild they keep a rather low profile, even though they are far from timid and withdrawn. It is a pity that they are not generally available in pet stores. Perhaps their less than striking plumage has had an effect on this, though they are very intelligent. A century ago they were commonly kept as house pets both in Europe and in their native land. Many of them had quite a vocabulary. Personally, I have never yet kept a white-eyed conure, but friends have told me that the beak of the

1

1. Hooded parrakeet, *Psephotus chrysopterygius dissimilis,* a very rare but beautiful bird that nests in a termite mound. 2. Yellow rosella, *Platycercus flaveolus.* This bird's attractive coloring also provides excellent protection, as it blends so well with the foliage. 3. Brown's rosella, or northern rosella, *Platycercus venustus,* is popular in collections. 4. Mallee ringneck parrot, *Barnardius barnardi.*

2

3

4

female is somewhat sturdier; no doubt this is a tip that could come in handy for a prospective buyer.

Good breeding results are repeatedly achieved in captivity, especially when the birds are given large breeding boxes measuring about 40 cm deep and 35 cm wide (16 x 14 inches). The bottom should be filled with moss that must be kept moist. Because this bird offers good breeding possibilities and is highly intelligent, it makes an excellent choice.

The subspecies *Aratinga leucophthalmus callogenys* is rarely offered for sale on the market and is a native of the tropical regions of eastern Ecuador and northeastern Peru.

Jandaya Conure (*Aratinga jandaya*)

Distribution: Northeastern Brazil.

Male and female: This very well known species has a golden yellow head with small red feathers. The throat area is also yellow. Breast and belly are a beautiful deep red, the back and wings green. Some of the wing feathers are blue. Rump red; tail green with yellow shine, margined with dark greenish blue. Brown eyes, black beak, and grayish black feet. Females and males that have not yet reached adulthood have less red on the face and breast; some even have green spots on the breast.

Length: 30-33 cm (12-13 1/5 inches); wings 14.8-16.4 cm (6-6 3/5 inches) tail 13-16 cm (5 1/5-6 2/5 inches).

Particulars: In the wild these birds do a great deal of damage, particularly to young tree plantations. They are unusually attached to each other. As a result, they can be kept in a community aviary with other parrakeet varieties and even their own species.

The female lays three to four eggs, which are hatched by both male and female. While they are breeding, they are not quite so easy-going; any birds that come too close to their nest will be greeted with raised neck feathers and abrupt little nods of the head. The breeding itself does not go as smoothly as is generally imagined. To increase our chances for good breeding results, a couple should be housed in a separate aviary. The breeding boxes they are given should measure 25 x 25 x 35 high (10 x 10 x 14 inches). The entrance hole should have a diameter of 8 cm (3 1/5 inches). The bottom should be covered with a thick layer (up to 8 cm) of moist peat moss over which we place a layer of twigs; the birds will gnaw these twigs to the proper shape.

The brooding period lasts 21 days. Once the young have come out of the egg, the parents should be given a plentiful amount of fruit and a rich variety of greens. A little change in the menu certainly would not hurt, particularly the fruits offered; I am thinking here of sweet apple, pineapple (small pieces), soaked raisins and currants, sweet soft pears, bananas, berries, etc. For greens we should offer them fresh twigs, chickweed, endive, and lettuce. For seeds offer: sunflower seeds, millet on the stalk, loose millet, some hemp, oats, canary seed, and a good brand of parrakeet seed. We should also include soaked seeds, such as weed and grass seeds, while soaked white bread and unripe grass seeds should be made available to them the year around, not just during the breeding period.

Strangely enough, these birds become accustomed to their new environment and the local weather quite quickly and will breed well and regularly if we stay within the above guidelines. For extra nutritional benefits we should supply them with fresh twigs and branches, different kinds of fruit (such as coconut cut into small pieces), corn, nuts, cherries, rye, etc. The fresh twigs are particularly important because these birds have an enormous gnawing instinct; virtually nothing is safe from them!

With regard to their gnawing activities, Houtenbos says in his book *Ik Kan Vogels Houden* (Sythoff, Leiden):

"The orange red and blood red breast and belly, against which the blue primaries rest, give this bird an important appearance, and make him very decorative in the aviary. But I personally have something against these birds, because they are very nervous. With the least amount of provocation they start up a racket that deafens the entire neighborhood. The male starts screeching first, and in a piercing tone. The female soon joins in, and together they give a screeching concert that any other bird would be hard pressed to beat. When my neighbor let his doves fly out at a set time every day, just the opening of the dovecot was enough to set off the jandayas. My wife needed only to shake out a single mat, and the jandayas would respond with a screeching number. Since our garden was quite small, it became necessary for me to get

A male (opposite) and female green rosella, *Platycercus caledonicus.* At 17 inches, the green rosella is the largest of the rosellas. This bird inhabits Tasmania and the larger islands of Bass Strait. The bold, noisy green rosella usually tolerates a close approach. The female green rosella differs from the male in that she is somewhat smaller and does not possess the wing-stripe.

237

1 and 2. Eastern rosella. 3. Young cockatiels. 4. Hybrid offspring of male rosella crossed with female red-rumped parrakeet. The first rosellas were bred in Spain in 1862, the first red-rumped in Britain in 1857 and in Germany in 1863.

4

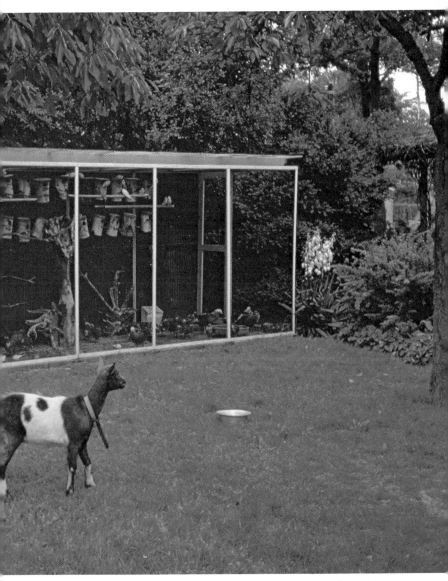

The author's aviary for budgerigars, offering all the comforts known to these birds in their natural habitat. Notice the attractive as well as sturdy construction of this aviary. Goat and birds get along just fine.

rid of my jandayas . . . at least if I wanted to live in some degree of peace . . .

"Their nervousness is also evidenced by their continuous gnawing at the perches. They constantly bite into the perches and attempt to reduce the aviary to ruins. It is therefore necessary to always have fresh branches available for them in the flight, preferably thick ones that will take them a while to get through. They can certainly go through a lot of them! It is a pity that the jandayas have this unattractive characteristic. If one is not careful, all that will be left of the aviary is splinters. Perhaps an aviary constructed with metal tubing would be ideal for these birds. However, if we make sure that they always have fresh branches hanging in the flight, this should take care of the problem as well."

So much for Houtenbos. Personally I believe he exaggerates a little, though I will admit that an aviary keeper with a small backyard may well have to deal with some irritated neighbors from time to time. There is still the possibility of taming the birds, though their screeching will never be given up completely. The reason that there are so few well tamed jandayas is because they are such ambitious breeders. Particularly in the States, there are thousands every year that are offered on the market, and they certainly enjoy a great deal of popularity. Their beautiful colors, lively behavior, and yearly family enlargements make good for what they possibly damage, and for the noise they may make.

The following species and subspecies all require basically similar care. They are all available from time to time.

The orange-fronted conure (*Aratinga canicularis eburnirostrum*) is generally available in every pet store at a relatively low price. These, too, are pretty bad screamers, but apart from that have a very pleasant nature and can be tamed quickly, particularly if we buy young birds; older birds generally cannot be tamed and rarely become good talkers. This species comes from western Mexico. In Central America a sister subspecies is found, namely *Aratinga canicularis canicularis,* and differs very little from *eburnirostrum.* They are often sold one for the other.

The golden-capped conure (*Aratinga auricapillo aurifrons*) looks a lot like the last described species and comes from southeastern Brazil. Its head is a little larger and the orange markings on the head are arranged differently. Instead of a wide orange band, this bird has a forehead band that ends in a little crown on top of the head. From Bahia to the easternmost area in Brazil comes a still somewhat larger subspecies, scientifically known as *Aratinga auricapillo auricapillo.*

The olive-throated conure (*Aratinga nana*) comes from Jamaica and is primarily green in color, olive-green on the throat and breast. There is some blue on the primary and secondary feathers, and a naked white periophthalmic ring. The bill is horn-colored, the iris orange, and the legs gray. One of its subspecies is *Aratinga nana astec,* often known as the Aztec conure. This bird differs from *nana* in that it is a little smaller and the colors are generally paler.

GENUS *NANDAYUS*

There is only one species that belongs to this genus, the nanday conure. This bird is so similar to the members of the genus *Aratinga* that it is really strange that it has been placed in a genus by itself.

Nanday Conure (*Nandayus nenday*)

Distribution: South America, particularly Paraguay.

Male and female: Primarily green. Blackish blue cap. Light green color traversed with black below the eye. Some blue on throat and upper breast. Flight feathers bluish black. Olive green tail with beautiful bluish black point; tail is very dark green underneath. Red thighs. Feet brownish pink; eyes reddish brown; bill blackish gray.

Length: 30-32 cm (12-12 4/5 inches); wings 18-19 cm (7 1/5-7 3/5 inches); tail 17 cm (6 4/5 inches).

Particulars: These birds are quite pleasant and can be kept in an aviary together with species belonging to the genus *Aratinga.* They become accustomed to their owner quite quickly. I know of a case where a nanday conure took seed out of his owner's hand after just two weeks.

Providing their accommodations are roomy, they will breed quite quickly. Do not hang the nesting boxes too high, because

A pair of Port Lincoln parrakeets; the female is the lower bird. In appearance, the two sexes differ only in the smaller head and beak size of the female.

Port Lincoln parrakeet, *Barnardius zonarius,* from the central and western parts of Australia. This bird is abundant in the wild. In captivity, it breeds well and is very hardy.

they like to sit on top of them and watch the world go by, while often making some very loud commentary! When the female is sitting on the eggs, the male may sit for hours on top of the box, and this time in silence. The female lays two to four eggs; both the male and female will sit on them. During the breeding season we should be sure to have plentiful amounts of the following: a rich variety of greens, fruits and berries, buds and twigs, almost ripe grain varieties (oats, rye, wheat, and hemp—not too much of the latter seed), corn on the cob and hard-boiled eggs cut into small pieces. Your birds should have calcium available to them, and soaked stale white bread and a salt block. If you have taken care of all these nutritional requirements, I am convinced that the breeding results will be completely successful. You will no doubt receive much pleasure from these birds, which can adjust very well to even a miserable climate. They can stay outside during the winter months though, of course, they must have a draft-free and dry shelter. My best results have always been obtained with a fairly roomy aviary housing just one couple. They are pleasant birds to have, with just one drawback: they have a loud, raucous call, to which they give voice with and without provocation. They are much too loud to keep indoors, and even in a small garden they can cause some irritation. Experience has shown, however, that once they are tamed and accustomed to their surroundings their screaming is considerably reduced. As a pet, they can be tamed very quickly and will take treats out of your hand in no time at all; they are also good talkers, though their vocabulary will never be more than limited.

GROUP II:
AFRO-ASIAN PARRAKEETS

This group of parrots and parrakeets includes some very well known species, such as the rose-ringed parrakeet (*Psittacula krameri manillensis*), but also the very popular genus of lovebirds (*Agapornis*). Because there is such a variety in shape, coloring and behavior, it would appear to be more sensible to describe the various genera and species in the individual descriptions rather than making some general remarks here; these remarks would only tend to be confusing.

We can say of the birds in this group, however, that they are relatively easy to keep and that most of them will breed regularly and well, providing their accommodations are not too small. Most of the birds are fairly tolerant of other species and will be a wonderful addition to a community aviary. A great combination, for example, would be three or four pairs of lovebirds, a pair of cockatiels, a pair of plum-headed parrakeets and rose-ringed parrakeets and/or moustached parrakeets housed in a roomy aviary measuring at least four meters long, three meters wide, and two and a half meters high (13x9x7½ feet). With this particular set-up we can expect several good breeding results every year, particularly when we plant a lot of shrubs in the aviary and disturb our birds as little as possible during the breeding season. There should also be a lot of shrubbery in front of the aviary, and we must certainly arrange for this if we have exotic birds in the aviary.

GENUS *PSITTACULA* (FORMERLY *PALAEORNIS*)

The trademarks of this genus would have to be the very long, slender tail and the pointed wings, giving these birds a fast flight. The female lays two to four eggs. They live mainly on seeds and fruit, and when kept in captivity, rice and corn should be added to their menu. Ornithologists recognize species in India, China, Sri Lanka, and Africa. These birds generally live harmoniously together in groups; after the breeding season a small troop, but often also large troops, separate themselves from the main group and go off to plunder the cornfields and rice paddies, doing a considerable

Barraband's parrakeet, also called superb parrakeet, *Polytelis swain-sonii*, needs a large, roomy, aviary to exercise its graceful ability for flight. Above is shown a young female; opposite is a male.

amount of damage. In the case of danger, or when they are being pursued, they hide in tree tops, well protected by the foliage. They prefer country traversed with rivers for use as drinking water. In the wild they can be seen skimming across the water's surface, much like swallows. Some species can be found living at higher levels: 1300-1400 meters (4900-5300 feet) above sea level. These parrakeets are very easy to care for and will repeatedly breed well. Some can learn to speak a few words. The very popular rose-ringed parrakeets are generally locally bred. Other birds, such as the moustached parrakeet, are still regularly imported and sold out quickly.

Naturally, new aviary inhabitants should be left undisturbed initially to allow them to become accustomed to their new surroundings, because they will still be quite timid and restless following their arrival. Some extra food on the ground would be a good idea. Once they have found the feeders, however, we can stop placing food on the ground. I would advise, if they are to be kept with exotic birds, choosing the sturdier types such as the larger cardinals; they may pose a danger for smaller varieties. They are generally tolerant with the larger parrakeet types, except during the breeding season.

The characteristic of this group is the colored (non-green) ring that starts at the throat and curves outward, turning down again at the neck. The body colors are generally shades of pastel, the primary color being a soft green. All the males have red beaks.

Rose-ringed Parrakeet (*Psittacula krameri manillensis*)

Distribution: India, Burma, Sri Lanka.

Male: Green, with a black collar and a black band around bill. Behind the black collar there is a red shine. Belly and under tail-coverts are yellowish green. Uppermost tail feathers are bluish green with yellow tips. Iris yellow-orange, beak red and feet black.

Female: Lacks the black collar and the red glow behind the collar. Young birds take their time in achieving their true colors. It will take at least two years before we can definitely determine their sex, while many cases may take as much as three years before the birds have their adult coloring. A written agreement with the seller allowing exchange would seem no luxury!

Particulars: These birds were introduced into Europe hundreds of years ago. Even the Greeks were familiar with them; they were mentioned by Archimedes (287-212 B.C.)

In the wild the female lays four eggs (28-33 mm x 22-22.6 mm); in captivity she sometimes lays five, but usually three to four. The female starts nest inspections very early in the year, around January, and will build up the nest by chewing into the proper shape the wood shavings and wood chips which you have placed in the nesting box. The box should measure 25 x 25 x 40 cm (10 x 10 x 16 inches), with an 8 cm (3 1/5 inches) diameter entrance. The female will take about three days to build up the nest. When all is in order, she will start to lay the eggs. Only the female sits on them. The male feeds both the female and later the offspring. After about a week the female will help in the feeding of the young. Feeding consists of stale soaked white bread and oven-dried bread, greens (lettuce, newly sprouted seeds, endive, chickweed, etc.), fruit (especially sweet fruit), hard-boiled eggs, sprouted seeds, oats, barley, canary seed, and a small amount of hemp. Once in a while we should provide some additional nutrition by offering ant-eggs. Since the breeding period starts very early in the year (January, February, March), they will need hard-boiled eggs, oats, greens, cuttlebone, and grit. After a good forty days the young will leave the nest and much resemble the female at that time.

Since rose-ringed parrakeets are very hardy birds, they can remain outside during the winter, as long as part of the aviary is covered and draft-free. Young birds that we have reared ourselves can learn to speak quite well, though a certain amount of isolation will be necessary here. In India some young birds are even reared by hand by the breeder; such birds are excellent cage birds once they are independent, with a generally remarkable repertoire of words and melodies. These are performed amid whistles and other tricks that will delight the owner.

They are ideal as aviary birds because they will breed easily and allow us to enjoy the utterly interesting breeding process. They should, however, be housed in an aviary of generous proportions, at least four to five meters (12-16 feet) long, because it has happened more than once that males housed in areas that were too small became sterile; this is the case with quite a few different par-

Jandaya conure, *Aratinga jandaya soltitialis,* from eastern Brazil. This bird is thought to be one of the most intelligent of the conures.

A pair of Barraband's parrakeets, *Polytelis swainsonii.* Notice the male's more colorful plumage.

1. Peach-fronted conures.
2. Aztec conure. 3. Red-fronted conure (left) and blue-crowned conure (right). 4. Tui parrakeet (left) and white-winged parrakeet, also called white-winged beebee (right). 5. Orange-fronted conure.

254

3

4

5

Yellow-fronted parrakeet, *Cyanoramphus auriceps.*

The green-winged king parrot, *Alisterus chloropterus,* from New Guinea, is so hardy that it can remain in an outdoor aviary throughout the year without heat.

257

rakeet varieties. In order to protect the aviary and any other wood-work, such as furniture and shrubbery, we should daily provide them with fresh willow twigs, etc. One of the interesting peculiarities of this species is that the female is definitely the dominant figure. During the winter months, or more accurately, outside the breeding season, the female will let her mate know in no uncertain terms that she wants no part of him! No serious wounds will come as a result of these little nips, so we need not concern ourselves over the aggressive behavior of the female.

Experience has shown that we should not allow the birds to start breeding too early in the year. The best time, in my opinion, is the middle of May. If we hang up the nesting boxes toward the end of March, the female will have ample opportunity to gnaw the nesting materials into the right shape. The love ritual is very interesting: he will hop around his mate in short little paces, making various little bows; he will also try to feed her. The hatching time is 22 to 24 days. Young independent birds should be placed in a roomy flight to promote their development into healthy and sturdy adults. They do not reach maturity until they are two to three years old. At that time the band on the males will have appeared, as we noted earlier. It is understood, no doubt, that the birds must not be allowed to breed until that time.

Some mutations have developed in the wild, similar to those that have taken place with the budgerigar, especially the blue, the lutino, and the yellow (in this case not "lutino-yellow"). These mutations have also been established in aviary birds, but the prices are prohibitive and these birds are rarely available on the market. A few years back, the Keston Foreign Bird Farm in England was successful in breeding the first albinos. In the no longer available magazine *Vogelrevue* (March 1964, No. 10), the well known breeder and author Edward J. Boosey, co-owner of the bird farm, wrote an interesting article about the albino form. According to Mr. Boosey, the first albinos were bred in July, 1963 as a result of the patience, skills, and knowledge of Mr. Bill Cummings. Boosey wrote: "Since the genetics of birds are passed down according to sex, the albino is a female, snow white in color, of course, with a pink beak." A correct male was also bred . . . in fact through the existing white female. He was a beautiful bird, blue in color (one of the parents—this must have been the father—was lutino).

Boosey continues: "We hope to breed an albino male in the not too distant future. This bird must, no doubt, be a beautiful specimen, because apart from the white plumage and the pink bill, he will also have a black and pink collar."

"It is not my intention, nor would it be possible in such a small article to go too deeply into the genetics. Therefore, I will limit it to just the statement of fact that the parents that created this albino had the same colors as the budgerigars which had the first albino. There is, however, this one difference, which is, no doubt, important to the breeder: budgerigars are fit for breeding very early in their lives, whereas Rose Ringed Parrakeets need to be at least three years old and even then we need a great deal of luck to be able to breed with them."

This is a long time, especially when compared with the three other color varieties that the Keston Foreign Bird Farm was the first to develop, namely the rainbow and the yellow masked budgerigars and the yellow red-rumped parrot, which were all able to breed after just one year. In the meantime it is interesting to speculate other possibilities in the color development of the rose-ringed parrakeet. The most obvious next color would be cobalt blue, which would certainly be a magnificent bird. This color could be followed with violet and a few other soft parrakeet colors, such as violet-blue with a pink bill and a white/black collar.

One would even have a tendency to venture further and imagine that there might also be possibilities for developing a blue, white-winged, "ringed parrakeet." This I feel would be impossible, since the original rose-ringed parrakeet is, after all, a plain green bird apart from the ring. In contrast to this, the original green budgerigar had color markings on the wings . . . only the under-side of their body is just one color.

The article mentioned above was republished in *Foreign Birds*. After publication, the editor received a letter from Mr. W. P. Bland, who stated that he thinks the male albino "ringed parrakeet" will have just a pink collar, as is the case with the lutinos. After having given this matter some additional thought, I have come to the conclusion that both Mr. Bland and myself are mistaken in this opinion for the following reason: in contrast to the lutino "ringed parrakeet" which belongs to the green series, the albino would have to belong to the blue series, which has a

Right and opposite: *Purpureicephalus spurius,* the red-capped parrakeet; this slender bird of the forest area of south-western Australia is very rare and difficult. A female is shown opposite; at right is a male.

black/white ring. If indeed the albino male does not have the black collar, he will not be able to be distinguished from the female, since the white collar will obviously not be visible. In connection with my speculation with regard to the appearance in the future of first shades of cobalt blue and later violet, Mr. Bland correctly points out that then first the "dark" factor will have to appear. So much for the article.

Closely related is *Psittacula krameri borealis* from India, Burma and southeastern China. Another subspecies, the African *Psittacula krameri krameri*, is not very frequently available on the market, though they can be found. Many of the subspecies are mixed up when they are sold because their differences are so slight. The African representative is somewhat smaller and more slender and lacks the pink around the collar ring. The blue in the plumage is either vague or missing altogether. No doubt their not so colorful plumage is the cause of their lesser popularity. The personality of these birds, however, is the same as that of their Indian counterparts. Ornithologists recognize yet two other races, namely: *Psittacula krameri parvirostris* (Ethiopia, Somalia and Sennar, Sudan) and *Psittacula krameri echo* (Mauritius—this bird is almost extinct, however).

Alexandrine Parrakeet (*Psittacula eupatria nipalensis*)

Distribution: Eastern Afghanistan south and east to Pakistan, north and central India, Nepal, Bhutan, and to Assam.

Male: Green; back of the head and cheeks greenish. Clearly visible collar and cheek markings, the collar red. Innermost tail feathers are bluish green with yellow-white tips. Gray eyes, encircled with red; deep red bill, and grayish brown feet.

Female: Very similar to the male. However, she lacks the black bands on the collar and cheeks. Before I get to the length data of these lovely birds, I would like to point out that this species can have a somewhat top-heavy appearance and does not look its best when it has just arrived from its native country, too often in a cage that is much too small, having damaged tail feathers as a result. Adult birds that have attained their adult size and are not afflicted with a damaged tail are truly beautiful birds which will enhance any aviary.

Length: 45-50 cm (18-20 inches); wings 19-20 cm (7 3/5-8 inches); tail 27-28 cm (10 4/5-11 1/5 inches).

Particulars: In the wild these birds live in small groups. Toward the evening, however, all these little groups get together to spend the night in the palm trees, separating again in the morning. A noteworthy fact is that once a group has been formed they generally always stay together. In contrast with the rose-ringed parrakeet, the Alexandrine parrakeet gnaws its own nest in the trees. The female lays two eggs (35.2 x 27.8 mm). They can be quite easily led to breeding, as long as they are housed in a roomy aviary by themselves. The nesting box should be about 45 x 40 cm (18 x 16 inches) and the entrance hole should have a diameter of at least 11-12 cm (4 2/5-4 4/5 inches).

It is a pity that these strong birds, which can remain outside during the winter providing they have a good shelter (to prevent the danger of freezing toes), are imported in such meager numbers. Admittedly there are more of them being imported during the last ten years, but their potential popularity has not reached its peak.

Only when kept in a cage can a young bird be taught to speak. In the aviary it is best to house these species in pair form to avoid fighting with other birds. They are tolerant of their own species except during the breeding cycle, but they are a nuisance and may even be dangerous toward small and large exotic birds. Other details run parallel with those of the rose-ringed parrakeet.

Other subspecies are: *Psittacula eupatria eupatria*—Sri Lanka and parts of India; this bird is smaller and its coloring is somewhat duller; *Psittacula eupatria siamensis*—Siam and Cochin China; *Psittacula eupatria avensis*—Burma and Cachar; *Psittacula eupatria magnirostris*—Andaman Islands; larger bill and less blue above the pink collar; *Psittacula eupatria wardi*—this bird is very likely extinct but lived (lives) on Silhouette Island.

Moustached Parrakeet (*Psittacula alexandri fasciata*)

Distribution: Southern China and India (see other races mentioned hereunder).

Male: Bright blue-gray head; black collar line. Cheeks outlined in black, flowing together at the black throat. Dark forehead, red collar, green back, green underside, and red breast. Tail blue with

The eggs of a turquoise parrot shown with a dime to show their relative size.

The turquoise parrot, *Neophema pulchella,* occurs in scattered areas only in southeastern Australia as it is becoming increasingly rare.

green seams. Green wings. Bright yellow shoulder markings. Yellow eyes. Upper mandible blackish red, lower mandible black. Grayish yellow feet.

Female: The wine red on the breast continues higher toward the throat and neck and the head is darker. The bill is black, but the upper mandible has an orange point. Young birds lack the red coloring and are generally grayer. Their bill is still black and it does not have an orange point.

Length: 37 cm (14 4/5 inches); wings 15-17 (6-6 4/5 inches); tail 19-23 cm (7 3/5-9 1/5 inches).

Particulars: Because of the fact that these birds sometimes land on rice paddies and cornfields in large flocks, they can do a great deal of damage. In the wild they build their nests as high as possible in the trees.

Because they are fairly quiet birds in captivity, they are often kept as a couple in a cage, particularly young birds. In the aviary, however, they can act quite wild and excited, which may cause them to be unsuitable for a community type aviary with fellow species and tropical birds. The watchword here is caution, and we suggest you place them in an aviary with others on a "trial basis," since you may very well have peaceful and quiet-natured birds. Several of these birds that I have kept in aviaries through the years were very quiet in just a few weeks and shared their homes willingly with their aviary-mates. If our birds are still young and we have a little patience, they can easily be taught to speak a few words. Their screeching becomes noticeably less once they are accustomed to their new housing and surroundings. They generally breed from March to May or July.

Fortunately these charming birds are regularly imported, and once in a while one might come across one of the other subspecies listed below. Their differences are so slight that one often can only determine the exact race if we know where the birds came from. Subspecies include: *Psittacula alexandri abbotti* (Andaman Islands); *Psittacula alexandri cala* (Simalur Island); *Psittacula alexandri major* (Tapa Islands); *Psittacula alexandri alexandri* (Java, Bali and to Borneo and the Kangean Islands); *Psittacula alexandri perionca* (Niss Island); *Psittacula alexandri dammermani* (Karimon, Java); and *Psittacula alexandri kangeanensis* (Kangean Islands).

Another collared parrakeet I would like to mention is the derbyan parrakeet (*Psittacula derbiana*), which could almost be a twin brother of the moustached parrakeet and comes from the isolated regions of southeastern Tibet and southwestern China. The difference here lies in the larger body and head. The head is bluish and the forehead has a black band that runs to the eyes; the remainder of head is purple with a black throat. Breast, underparts, and under wing-coverts purple, back and wings green. The red upper mandible ends in a yellow point and the lower mandible is black. The eyes are yellowish, the feet greenish gray. Personally, I think this is one of the most beautiful birds of the moustached parrakeet group and feel that every serious-minded parrakeet breeder should have a place for this bird, even though breeding results are not very easily attained . . . but then, if everything took care of itself, there would be very little challenge left in our hobby.

Long-tailed Parrakeet (*Psittacula longicauda longicauda*)

Distribution: Malaysia.

Male: Green; crown dark green. Back of head, neck, and cheeks are red. Clearly visible black "moustache." Blue marking on rump. Center tail feathers greenish blue. Yellow eyes; upper mandible blood red; lower mandible is black; gray feet.

Female: Her "moustache" is dark green instead of black. Back of head is green. Both upper and lower mandibles are black. Tail is about 4 cm (1 3/5 inches) shorter than that of the male.

Length: 40 cm (16 inches); wings 15 cm (6 inches); tail 23-25 cm (9 1/5-10 inches).

Particulars: This bird is not so generally well known and can be quite wild immediately after arrival. Unfortunately this trait rarely disappears completely. The long-tailed parrakeet generally starts to breed in April, and the nesting boxes should be hung up around mid-April; the female will still need some time to gnaw the wood chips and such into the proper shape for the nest. You will see that this purposely delays the beginning of the breeding season by a few weeks, and we do this for the purpose of preventing egg-binding, which quite often afflicts the females of this species.

In the wild these attractive birds live in large flocks. They love to fly and are quite active by nature. This is why they feel most

1

2

1. Bourke's parrakeet, *Neopsephotus bourkii*, from southern and central Australia. This species is a birdlover's favorite. It is a friendly little bird that can easily be housed in a mixed collection. 2. Female Bourke's parrakeet. 3. The pinkness of the chest and abdominal region shows this Bourke's parrakeet to be a male.

3

4

1. Baby elegant parrots. 2. Port Lincoln parrot. 3. Turquoise parrot, male. 4. Red-rumped parrakeet, male. 5. Pale-headed rosella.

5

SEED GERMINATION requires any birdseed which is fresh. You also require (1) an aluminum tray, a strainer, bowl, and plastic wrap. The strainer must fit into the bowl and be able to support itself (2) on the rim. Fill the strainer with the birdseed (3), and rinse it under running water until it is thoroughly clean (4). Allow it to soak for about a day (5) in the bowl. Change the water as frequently as convenient, but at least once every 12 hours. Then pour the dampened seed onto the tray (6) and spread the seed uniformly (7). Mix in any mold-inhibiting substance (Moldex) and cover the seed to keep the moisture in, but not to stop air from getting to the seed (8, 9). If you want to grow *grass* from the seed you can use earth (10), sprinkle it with seed (11), mix the seed with the earth (12), sprinkle lightly with water (13) and store in a warm, dark place (14). The seed used with earth can either be soaked for a while (see above 1 through 5), or straight from the box.

273

comfortable in an aviary that measures at least four meters (12 feet) long. We should be sure to keep one couple in an aviary, because a bird by himself can cause a lot of problems. I once had a male by himself that constantly flew around the aviary, flapping his wings, and repeatedly injured his head on the wire. When I arranged for a female to join him, they became the best of friends within the week and reared two nests of three and five young respectively (breeding season 1969/70). Therefore, I would emphasize the advice to only keep these birds in pairs; this is almost certain insurance that you will not have to put up with restless, constantly flying birds that give voice to deafening screeches the entire day long and bring angry neighbors to your door! When kept in pairs they are quite peaceful and may sit for hours on the roof of the nesting box or a thick perch, watching the life around them.

They got their name from their slender long tail, of which the two center feathers are the longest. These are blue in color and can only be clearly seen when the bird spreads his tail. Other subspecies are: *Psittacula longicauda defontainei*—Natuna Islands, Rhio, and surrounding islands. Paler in color than *longicauda longicauda; Psittacula longicauda modesta*—from Engano Island, and also paler in coloring; *Psittacula longicauda nicobarica*—Nicobar Islands; and *Psittacula longicauda tytleri*—Andaman Islands.

Plum-Headed Parrakeet (*Psittacula cyanocephala*)

Distribution: India.

Male: Plum-colored head and wings; black seam around the head, followed by a bluish green band. Dark green wings. Balance of body is light green. Innermost tail feathers bluish green, outer tail feathers green with light yellow tips. Brown eyes; yellowish white bill; grayish brown feet.

Female: Her head band is constantly lighter and the red shoulder marking is missing. Her head is grayish purple. Young birds reach their adult colors after a full two years. Since young males look like females before these two years have elapsed, we need to be very careful when purchasing these birds.

Length: 35-37.5 cm (14-15 inches); wings 13-14 cm (5 1/5-5 3/5 inches); tail 22-23 cm (8 4/5-9 1/5 inches).

Particulars: These birds are regularly offered for sale on the market and stand out for their pleasant nature, also displayed toward fellow species and not too small exotic birds. In their native land they live both in the jungles and the cultivated areas. They can cause quite a lot of damage. Outside of the breeding period, they live in small groups. They are skillful fliers and live on bananas, other fruit, seeds, and rice. When kept in captivity it is sometimes difficult to accustom them to a seed menu (oats, hemp, canary seed, grain, and various grass seeds, in addition to a good brand of parrakeet seed for large species). We should be sure to offer them plenty of greens, young buds, eggs, oven-dried bread, mealworms, and ant-eggs. The latter two are particularly important when there are young in the nest.

Before the birds commence breeding, we must cover the bottom of the nesting box, which should measure 20 cm x 30 cm (8 x 12 inches) with an 8 cm (3 1/5 inches) diameter entrance opening, with wood chips and sawdust. The female lays two to six eggs (27-29.7 x 19.8-23.6 mm) which only she will hatch. The male will feed the female from his crop during the breeding cycle. After about 23 days the young will come out of the egg. Strangely enough, the female will remain inside the nesting box for another 8 to 20 days after the young have come out of the egg, while a very busy daddy feeds both wife and children. As already mentioned, the eggs take about 23 days to hatch, but it may take several days longer because the eggs are often laid over a considerable time-span. So don't be too quick to throw out apparently unfertilized eggs! The breeding period is from October to March or the middle of April.

Since acclimation can cause some difficulties, I would advise against buying birds during the end of December through the middle of February; it would be better to wait until spring. If you have already bought them during this time, however, it would seem obvious that we not encourage them to breed during this time.

Their not unpleasant song has contributed to their popularity among fanciers, who successfully and frequently breed them. It is unfortunate that there seems to be a tendency to import more males than females. Since these birds do not achieve their adult coloring until they are two years of age, it would be sensible to

An Australian king parrot, *Alisterus s. scapularis.* The male pictured here displays a brilliant red plumage.

Golden mantled rosella, *Platycercus eximius cecilae,* also known as the Splendid rosella.

make an arrangement with the seller that will allow you to exchange one of your birds should they not form a true pair. Naturally, with all this exchanging and waiting to see if we are, indeed, in the possession of a true pair, a lot of time is wasted before we can begin some fruitful breeding. The question that would arise is: are there no differences that would speed up this process and allow a more accurate determination of the sexes? There is, unfortunately, very little difference to be discerned; perhaps the heads of the young birds are somewhat grayer in color than birds that are ready for breeding, but that is the only difference. You will probably say that that is not much to go on, and I will have to admit that caution and a trust in the seller are the two points that we should keep in mind.

Some ornithologists recognize two subspecies, and although they are both a little smaller in size, the coloring differences are barely discernible. *Psittacula cyanocephala cyanocephala* lives in the jungles of southern India and Sri Lanka and *Psittacula cyanocephala bengalensis* makes its home in the northern areas of India and Bengal.

Besides being fairly good breeders, plum-headed parrakeets are all quite pleasant singers. Breeding results are obtained only when a couple has an aviary to themselves; the aviary should measure at least four meters in length and be three meters in width (12 x 9 feet). Rest is very important for the birds during the breeding period and for the success of the clutch; these parrakeets are particularly timid and frighten very quickly during this time. A plentiful number of shrubs both inside and in front of the aviary does much to alleviate their jumpiness.

Finally, I would like to point out that a few lutinos have been bred but are rare and therefore expensive. Perhaps due to the fact that the plum-headed parrakeet does not breed *that* easily, we have not yet achieved the "color breeding" stage which is possible, as an example, with the rose-ringed parrakeet.

Malabar Parrakeet (*Psittacula columboides*)

Distribution: Southern southwestern India.

Male: Green; upper body and head gray. There is a black band at the eyes and throat that joins at the neck. A pale blue band follows this and becomes paler green at the throat. There is often a little blue on the forehead and above the cheeks and a greenish color around the eyes. Breast, flanks, and shoulders are a soft gray with a pinkish reflection. Wings and tail blue, wings paler at the tips, giving the impression that the coloring of the wings is scalloped. Tail feathers are tipped in yellow. Under tail-coverts are yellowish green.

Female: Has a black bill but is missing the band as well as the pink reflection in the gray areas, although some of them do show a vague pink shine.

Length: 36-38 cm (14 2/5-15 1/5 inches); wings 15 cm (6 inches); tail 24 cm (9 3/5 inches).

Particulars: These birds live together peacefully in small flocks and go hunting together as well. Consequently, they do quite a job of ransacking fruit trees. In their native country they are, unfortunately, becoming quite rare, and it would seem to be time that the government there undertakes steps to protect them. The female lays four eggs in a nest made in tree cavities made by woodpeckers and such. In the aviary they will use regular nesting boxes. The breeding period is January to March or the beginning of April.

I do not feel that this bird makes a very suitable aviary inhabitant because its nature is very quiet and it moves around so little. They can also be quite troublesome toward fellow species and small exotic birds and may try to bite them. Ideally, a couple can be kept in an aviary measuring 2 x 2 x 1½ meters (6 x 6 x 4½ feet) or in a roomy cage; then they are very sweet. The chances for breeding results are quite good. I feel this bird deserves an honorable place in the tree of birds, not only because of its lovely coloring and attractive build, but because it is fairly rare in its home land. Certainly rarity alone should give fanciers a satisfying challenge. It would not be the first time that bird fanciers have prevented the extinction of some species, in spite of the unkind remarks that are often aimed at them by bird conservationists and similar societies.

The Malabar parrakeet was previously known scientifically as *Psittacula peristerodes.*

There are a few other species belonging to the genus *Psittacula,* but they are rarely offered for sale on the market. For the sake of completeness I will mention them for you.

1 and 2. Malee ringneck parrakeet, *Barnardius barnardi*. 3. Cloncurry parrakeet, *Barnardius barnardi macgillivrayi*. 4. Northern rosella, *Platycercus venustus*, also known as Brown's rosella.

3

4

1. Blue-winged parrotlet (*Forpus* species). 2. Green conure. 3. Cactus conure. 4. Moustached parrakeet, male.

1. Blue-winged parrakeet, *Neophema chrysostoma.* These social birds have been observed in groups of as many as twenty birds. 2. A swift parrakeet, *Lathamus discolor,* named for its ability for swift flight. 3. Stanley, or western, rosella, *Platycercus icterotis,* with a pair of Scarlet-chested parrots, *Neophema splendida.*

2

3

The slaty-headed parrakeet (*Psittacula himlayana himalayana*) makes its home in the northern regions of India in the Himalaya Mountains. It looks a lot like the plum-headed parrakeet and is the same size as the rose-ringed parrakeet. The male has a red bill, a slate colored head, and red markings on the shoulders. The tail feathers are tipped in white. The rest of its description parallels that of the rose-ringed and plum-headed parrakeets. The female lacks the wine-red shoulder markings and her head is a paler gray. The subspecies *Psittacula himalayana finschii* originates in Burma and India. This race is also rarely offered for sale, and when they are often pass for plum-headed or rose-ringed parrakeets. It is, therefore, well worthwhile to closely inspect all the birds in a particular collection; perhaps one may be lucky and find one of the rarer species.

The emerald-collared parrakeet (*Psittacula calthorpae*) is smaller than the rose-ringed parrakeet and the tail is shorter, giving this bird a plumper appearance. This species comes from Sri Lanka but is rarely offered for sale. The male has a red bill and a gray head that displays green reflections and spots; some green is clearly visible around the eyes and the collar region as well. There is a broad black band around the throat and a green tint in the neck. The back is gray, slowly becoming cobalt blue, then becoming vaguer again at the tail. The wings show colors ranging from pastel green to olive and dark green at the edges. Females have a black bill and are generally duller in color.

Less known are the following:

Intermediate parrakeet (*Psittacula intermedia*): we still do not know exactly where in India this bird makes its home. The fact that this bird is very rare does not help studies aimed at deterining its native region.

Then there is (or was) Newton's parrakeet (*Psittacula exsul*), of which it is surmised that there are very few surviving members or it is extinct altogether; it lived (lives) on the island of Rodriguez.

Finally there is Blyth's parrakeet (*Psittacula caniceps*), a very sturdy bird, larger than the rose-ringed parrakeet, with a long tail and a gray head. The beak is red and there is a black band on the forehead. This species gives the impression of wearing some sort of triangular moustache. This bird, too, is very rarely available for purchase.

GROUP III: AUSTRALIAN BROAD-TAILED PARRAKEETS

This very well known group includes some eighty species that live in, among other places, Australia and New Zealand. Their beautiful plumage has made them big favorites among bird fanciers and breeders, and they are, as consequence, kept and bred by many and sold for fairly high prices.

Their tail is long and lovely, as are the wings. The generic name of the main genus, *Platycercus,* means literally "broad-tailed" and has given the group its nickname of broad-tailed parrots. They live in large flocks on the steppes, such as the deserts of central Australia, and search for grass seeds after the rainy season. Food requirements in the aviary are: grass seeds, oats, panicum millet, berries, apples, grapes, pears, cherries, and fresh buds and twigs (lime tree, hazel, elder, willow, various fruit trees, etc.). Also greens in various forms, such as chickweed, lettuce, seedlings, etc. They also appreciate ant-eggs, hard boiled eggs, and soaked stale bread. In the breeding period we could give them cream on a slice of stale bread that has been soaked in milk.

Because of their pleasant and tolerant attitude (even more-or-less so during the breeding season) they can be kept in most cases in community aviaries. Some species can learn to talk very well and clearly. Their song is pleasant to the ear. They build their nests in holes and cracks of various trees. The average nesting box should have the following dimensions: 35-40 cm. high, 25-28 cm. wide (14-16 x 10-11 inches); entrance opening has a diameter of 8 cm (3 1/5 inches). More pertinent data can be found under the individual species.

GENUS *POLYTELIS*

Around 1830 a few birds were seen along the Murrumbidgee and Murray Rivers that were profoundly different from the already established rosella species. One of the discoverers, among others, was J. Stuart, who thought these birds were so beautiful that he included this in their scientific name: *polytelis* means beautiful and gorgeous in Greek. (Stuart also discovered the regent parrot). Many years later, in 1865, Fr. Waterhouse dis-

1. This monk or Quaker parrakeet, *Myiopsitta monachus,* is only 24 days old. 2. A young sun conure, *Aratinga solstitialis.* 3. A young Scarlet-chested parrot, *Neophema splendida.* This bird tends to stay in pairs or small parties of less than ten birds. 4. This female Bourke's parrakeet, *Neopsephotus bourkii,* is feeding her young in the wild.

3

4

covered a third species, the well known princess parrot, which belongs to the subgenus *Spathopterus.*

These birds can be identified by their long slender tails, which have two extremely long center feathers. Male and female are not identical, so the buyer will have no problem in differentiating between the sexes. This genus has yet one other advantage over the other Australian broad-tailed genera: these birds live in regions that make it possible for them to adapt quite well to colder climes. Consequently, all three species are excellent choices for keeping in the aviary, even during the winter months. We will, however, have to watch out for two tendencies pertinent to these species: eye infections and lameness. Both points are also made in Dr. Groen's book on Australian parrakeets. Should we happen to get an imported bird in our possession, we must not immediately place this bird in an outside aviary, but gradually accustom him to food and climate. Specimens bred in Europe and Japan must never be placed into damp or drafty aviaries. The aviary must always be equipped with a wind- and rain-free night shelter. The three representatives would do better if placed in a lightly heated area inside during the winter months.

Princess Parrot (*Polytelis alexandrae*)

Distribution: The deep inland areas of Australia, from the central western and northwestern regions to the northern parts of South Australia.

Male: Crown and area around the eye are a vague sea-blue. Yellow/gray/green at the back of the head and neck, shoulders, and back. Throat, breast, and part of the cheeks are pinkish red. Bright sky blue rump. Pinkish red feathers around the feet. Light yellow-green on underside and wings; flight feathers are darker. Yellow green tail margined in blue/green; tips of tail feathers are white. Light orange eyes, encircled with red (not in the female); red bill, brown feet.

Female: The blue in the female is grayish blue, particularly the center feathers of the tail, but often the entire tail is shorter and deep red on the inside, margined in black. Bill is not as red as in the male; there is less violet on the rump.

Length: 35-36½ cm (14-14 3/5 inches); wings 17-17½ cm (6 4/5-7 inches); tail 20-23 cm (8-9 1/5 inches).

Offspring: Not until they are six months old do they start to show differences that will enable the determination of their sex. The eyes will give the first indication, followed by a bluish haze on the head of the males.

Particulars: Although in 1959 I wrote in my book *Parkieten en Papegaaien* (Thieme, Zutphen) that I thought it was a shame that these lively birds could only be seen sporadically in zoos and bird parks, they are now commonly held by a great many bird fanciers. Thanks to these bird breeders, we can expect these birds to be saved from extinction, because, as I remarked in my earlier book, the princess parrot is almost as good as extinct in Australia, despite excellent governmental efforts to protect this species. In January, February, and March of 1966, I accompanied a few ornithologists to Alice Springs on a biological study trip, and we saw a group of princess parrots on three different occasions (8, 12, and 15 birds respectively). This does cast a shadow of doubt on Dr. Groen's remark that: "there have only been three published observations of princess parrots in the wild during the last 25 years." Groen wrote in 1962: "The last published observation is from 1953, when John Callaby saw this species in the northeastern region of Western Australia, 80 miles north of Mindawindi. It is difficult to say whether we should assume from the above that the princess parrot is, indeed, becoming extinct. The limited number of observations in the wild may be partly due to the fact that these birds live a rather nomadic existence, spread over an enormous area in a continent which is only sparsely populated."

Although Dr. Groen expressed himself rather carefully, he is, nevertheless, mistaken. Recent publications about this species indicates that they are scarce, but are not seen as seldom as he would have us believe. In the latest edition of *What Bird Is That?* by Neville W. Cayley (edited by A.H. Chrisholm, K.A. Hindwood and A.R. McGill), 1964—an unchanged reprint from the third edition in 1959—nothing is mentioned about the population density; the authors only say: ". . . in pairs or small flocks, ususally frequenting belts of timber near watercourses. The species is nomadic, moving over long distances in searching for the seeds of various grasses, chiefly spinifex. Both flocks and pairs maintain a continuous chatter when perched in trees."

1. Two very young derbyan parrakeets, *Psittacula derbiana*. These birds come from the high mountain regions of southeastern Tibet and southwestern China. 2. A young Port Lincoln parrakeet, *Platycercus z. zonarius.* 3. Rock pebbler, *Polytelis anthopeplus*, also known as the regent parrot, roosts in tall trees at night near river banks or some other source of water and travels great distances daily to feed. 4. Sun conure, *Aratinga solstitialis.*

3

4

That these birds are rare is an open question. However, everything is being done by the Australian government to protect these birds from extinction, which is no small task and, as we saw, entirely possible. The biggest problem in establishing efficient controls lies in the fact that these birds lead a wanderer's life and therefore are difficult to follow; should they be around Alice Springs in a certain year (such as in 1966), the next year may find them hundreds of miles further inland. Since they live in areas where people seldom tread, control is extremely difficult.

These lovely parrots, which breed in tree hollows and tree trunks usually in close proximity to small rivers or creeks, live in small groups or in pairs. They seem to breed as well in captivity as they do in the wild. Mating is preceded by an interesting ritual where the couple press their cheeks together and "embrace" each other with their wings.

The female usually lays four white eggs (4 to 6 in the wild), with a one- or two-day interval between each egg. During the breeding cycle the male will feed the female. In the wild the breeding period takes place from September through December, but it may start earlier or end later, depending on the region where the birds are living at the time and on the ripeness of the spinifex seeds (spinifex is a little like canary seed). The hatching period is about three weeks. We should give them mulched wood for use as nesting material, such as from willow or poplar. Place this in the nesting box yourself, along with grass, wool, dry grass, and hay.

During the breeding season supply them with plentiful amounts of greens, hemp, and canary seed. . .the young will be reared mainly on these foods. The male will feed the young as well. After 35 days the young will leave the nest, and after about 15 months they will be ready for breeding. Yet I am sure that every experienced fancier will agree that we cannot always count on success with our breeding attempts. The female will most likely start to lay eggs, but will leave the nest with the least provocation and not return until all is quiet or safe again. It is this returning to the nest that does not always proceed with enough care on the part of the female, so many a time one or more eggs will be broken. If we wish to enhance our chances for success, we will have to allow breeding to take place under very quiet and peaceful conditions. Inside the nesting box affix a few horizontal pieces of wood or a piece of wire that will serve as a ladder, facilitating the coming and going of the female. Quite a lot of fanciers allow the breeding to take place in hollow tree trunks. Experience has taught the breeder that both nesting boxes and tree trunks should be placed at an angle of about 45°. The female will then no longer tend to just plop back onto her eggs when she returns to the nest, but will be forced to first step onto the back wall and then walk along the wire that we have hung against this wall to reach her eggs. Quite a number of breeders use an incubator. As they are laid, the eggs fall through a coarse wire onto a thick layer of sawdust so they will not be damaged. The box has a double bottom so the egg can be easily taken away and replaced with a stone or clay egg of the same size. When the clutch is complete we remove the wire bottom. If after two weeks it appears that the female is doing a good job of sitting on the eggs, we can return the real ones to the nest, as in this way we will not have to cope with the problem of rearing the babies. If, however, we are planning to rear the fledglings ourselves, we do not use an artificial breeder but good foster parents; the eggs will remain fresh for quite a while, providing we keep them in a dark place.

In order to prevent the males from becoming sterile, we should house our pairs in large aviaries; personally I think that a length of six to seven meters (18-22 feet) is the minimum. With some luck and a little skill, a pair will generally not present you with too many problems; two clutches per year can be considered quite normal. As previously mentioned, birds are ready for breeding when they are fifteen months old.

It is interesting to know that cross-breeding has taken place with the rose-ringed parrakeet (excellent foster parents!), the regent parrot, and the well known red-winged parrot, while the first blue mutation was achieved in 1951 in Australia but never definitely established, so that the future of this color is not yet certain, unfortunately.

Regent Parrot (*Polytelis anthopeplus*)

Distribution: Australia: northern parts of Victoria and bordering areas of New South Wales to the low eucalyptus growth areas of southeastern South Australia. They are also found in south-

1. Lutino rose-ringed parrakeet, *Psittacula krameri manillensis;* this species inhabits Ceylon, Rameswaram Island and parts of India. 2. Redrump parrakeets, *Psephotus haematonotus,* in an aviary. 3. The author's aviaries, providing a natural and comfortable enclosure for captive birds. 4. Jandaya conure, *Aratinga jandaya.* 5. A well constructed outdoor aviary.

4

5

western Australia to the east of Esperance.

Male: Yellowish green. Grass-green back with dark markings. The wings are yellow with black flight feathers and black wing curves. Wing-coverts are red, margined in yellow. Tail black with a blue shine, deep black on underside. Red eyes and beak; grayish brown feet.

Female: Where the male is yellow (or yellow-green) the female is green. Red stripes on the tail. Deep dark green on top side of tail. Young birds resemble the female. After about six months the males will start to color up, and after eighteen months they will have achieved adult coloring.

Length: 35-40 cm (14-16 inches); wings 17-19 cm (6 4/5-7 3/5 inches); tail 20-22 cm (8-8 4/5 inches).

Particulars: A noteworthy fact about these birds is that the young have black eyes until the first molting, which takes place at around eighteen months of age; after that the eyes are red.

Regent parrots are very pleasantly natured birds that are regularly offered for sale on the market. They are even pleasant toward small exotic species such as red-eared waxbills, zebra finches, and fire finches. They might prove to be less tolerant toward fellow species, particularly if they are housed in a somewhat small aviary and during the breeding period.

The female lays four eggs (32-32.3 x 23-23.2 mm); in the wild she may lay anywhere from four to six eggs. In the wild, these birds live on, among other things, wild honey, blossoms leaves, seeds, and fresh buds. They prefer to choose tree hollows in which to build their nests, ideally along the edge of large rivers. During the evening they like to fly over the water and their screeching call can be heard miles away. Outside of the breeding time, they live together in small groups of ten to twelve birds and can often be found in rubber plantations. They do not, however, cause any damage.

This gorgeous bird, which is ready for breeding after two years, sometimes sooner, has a subspecies living in Western Australia. This is *Polytelis anthopeplus westnalis,* which has more green in its plumage. The coloring of this subspecies is also very lovely, as evidenced by his Greek name, which means "coat of flowers." Regent parrots have been bred in Europe for a considerable time, well before bird breeding became a fairly common hobby. While this bird was first described in 1831 by Lear, in 1865 a Danish breeder reported the first successful breeding results, followed soon by others in England and Germany. Belgium, too, was not to be left behind; the Netherlands, for some unknown reason, has not shown very much interest in the regent parrot. Personally, I consider this bird to be utterly beautiful, particularly in a roomy outdoor aviary and it will even become hand-tame with good care. Since regent parrots by nature breed high up, we should hang our nesting boxes as high as possible. Take care *not* to leave a space for the birds to sit on top, as they will spend much time during the day on the roof and in this manner might fall prey to any prowling cats or other animals that are dangerous to aviary birds. We should hang a few different types of aviary boxes that should measure at least 25 x 25 x 65 cm (10 x 10 x 26 inches) with an entrance opening of at least 8 cm (3 1/5 inches). In the wild these birds breed from September to December, as high as possible in the eucalyptus trees; in the aviary we should not give them access to the nesting boxes until the middle of April.

As we already said, these birds generally live in small groups, possess a very fast flight capacity, and love to sit in the top of eucalyptus trees and sing for hours! Cross-breeding has been established with the princess parrot, the superb parrot, and the red-winged parrot.

Superb Parrot (*Polytelis swainsonii*)

Distribution: Australia: mainly along the Murray and Murrumbidgee Rivers in New South Wales and bordering regions, including the deep northern areas of Victoria and stretching out to above the Castlereagh River and the Lanchland River, even to the east of Sydney. This area is the smallest territory of any of the Australian broad-tailed birds.

Male: Green, bright light yellow forehead, throat, and cheeks. Red blotch on the throat. Flight feathers are blue; the lovely tail is green, margined in blue; underside of the tail is black. Orange-yellow eyes. Red bill, brown feet.

Female: Her green coloring is less sharp than that of the male. No yellow on the head. Thighs show some red feathers. Some pink underneath the tail. Brown eyes.

Length: 32-36 cm (8-9 inches); wings 16-17.7 cm (6 2/5-7 inches);

5

6

1. A male many-color parrakeet, *Psephotus varius.* 2. Many-color parrakeet, female. 3. A young female red-rump parrakeet, *Psephotus haematonotus.* 4. Red-rump parrakeet, male. 5. Princess Alexandra parrakeet, *Polytelis alexandrae.* 6. Red fronted parrakeet, *Cyanoramphus novaezelandiae.* 7. Yellow fronted parrakeet, *Cyanoramphus auriceps.* 8. Australian king parrakeet, *Alisterus chloropterus.*

7

8

tail 20-23 cm (8-9 1/5 inches).

Offspring: The young very much resemble the female; the males have some red at the thighs too, and some males retain this color, even after the first molting, though this is unusual. With a little experience, one can generally identify the sexes after the initial molting by the yellow-green heads of the males and the gray-green heads of the females. There are some brown feathers on the throat of the male, which will later be replaced by the red band. These brown feathers are not present on the females . . . at the most a brownish shadow will remain after the first molting. After a year they will attain adult coloring.

Particulars: In spite of the fact that these birds are rather expensive, they are kept by a great many bird fanciers, both in Australia and elsewhere. Their peaceful nature has, no doubt, contributed to their popularity. Breeding is altogether possible, but then it is advisable to house them in a roomy aviary by themselves without fellow species or other birds. Although they breed only once a year in the wild (from September to November) on four to six eggs, in the aviary they may breed twice. We should give them a deeply hollowed tree trunk in which to build their nest and cover the bottom of this hollow with mold, sawdust, and wood chips. In the wild these birds prefer a tree hollow, preferably as high off the ground as possible, just like the previous species. These parrots rarely live in pairs, but rather in small groups (eight to ten birds), particularly outside of the breeding period, though some will also maintain their group living during the breeding season. They can generally be found in close proximity to water, with low wood and grass growths. They feed mainly on grass seeds and other seeds from plants, as well as on nectar and greens from eucalyptus trees, etc. In other words, they live mostly on the ground.

In captivity, we should feed them with a good seed mix prepared for large parrakeet varieties and plenty of canary seed and hemp as well. Should the birds start to breed, I feel you would be well advised to leave them alone and forget about exercising any controls, because many a clutch has been lost that way. Leave them to their own affairs, make sure they have plenty of food and water, and keep any animals and children far away from the aviary. It is best, of course, not to give the breeding couple the company of any other aviary inhabitants.

Although they have a hardy constitution, we should try to see that they do not get problems with their feet and eyes. Lameness, in particular, is a fairly common affliction of this species. Although a great many authors would have us keep these birds outside even during the winter months, I would like to advise that they be brought indoors into a lightly heated area to prevent cold and consequently lame feet. Most birds that have suffered from this are no longer suitable for breeding. Another area of vulnerability with these birds is the eyes, so watch for anything out of the ordinary.

Cross-breeding can be done with the other two species of *Polytelis* as well as with the red-winged parrot, the king parrots, and the eastern rosellas. As I mentioned earlier, I am not personally in favor of these attempts and would like to appeal to the serious-minded parrakeet breeder to cross-breed different species as little as possible. The resultant offspring are not usually better or more attractive, and from an ornithological point of view the pure species is both more valuable and more interesting, especially because some of the parent species are so rare in the wild.

In 1867 these birds were first transported to London; in 1900 in England the first breeding results were obtained. They are very pleasant birds and can be tamed quite easily, though they will never be as affectionate as the regent parrot. With this species, as with the others, we will have to be prepared for their rather loud voices. Young birds that are kept by themselves can be taught to speak a few words; some specimens can even learn to whistle a few simple melodies.

GENUS *ALISTERUS*

I am placing the following species under this genus, with a certain amount of reserve, because it is still generally supposed that these species should fall under the genus *Aprosmictus,* which consists of nine species plus subspecies. Even the most recent edition of Cayley's book, *What Bird Is That?,* which I feel is the trend-setting standard work on Australian birds, says nothing about this classification. Only Dr. Groen wants to definitely see this genus, with its three species and several subspecies, divorced from the genus *Aprosmictus.* I agree with Dr. Groen entirely, and on a

1

2

1. Aviary under repair. The bird-owner must be prepared to handle minor repairs from time to time. 2. Double row of breeding pens. 3. These outdoor aviaries blend harmoniously with their immediate surroundings.

3

purely ornithological basis. It is not within the scope of this book to go in depth into these desired changes in the systematic classification of birds. This genus has three species and about ten subspecies. Unfortunately, all but one of these representatives are unknown to the aviary keeper and are even rarely seen in large zoos and bird parks. These birds live in Australia, on West Irian (formerly Dutch New Guinea), and on several East Indonesian islands (Amboina, Ceram, Buru, to name a few).

Australian King Parrot (*Alisterus scapularis scapularis*)

Distribution: Eastern Australia, from Cooktown to southern Victoria.

Male: Red on throat, head, and underside. The rump is blue, continuing to the uppermost tail feathers; balance of tail is dark brown, greenish black on top. Wings and back are a dark grass-green; brown eyes, with yellow iris; pinkish red beak, edged in black; gray feet.

Female: Where the male has red colors, the female is light grass green, except for her belly, which is pinkish red. The beak is gray-black. Young birds resemble the female, though the bill is yellow. After six months the sexes can be distinguished because the males will then have a shining beak, and a great deal less gray in the plumage than the females. After a year the males will start to show red on the breast and head, but it takes still another year before their adult coloring is complete and they are ready for breeding.

Length: 36.5-40 cm (14 3/5-16 inches); wings 19-22.7 cm (7 3/5-9 inches); tail 18-21 cm (7 1/5-8 2/5 inches).

Particulars: This species makes a beautiful cage bird, but if breeding results are desired a very roomy aviary will be absolutely essential. The king parrot well deserves its name. It likes to take a bath every day; in the wild they can often be seen splashing either themselves or each other at the river's edge. We were lucky enough to experience this several times during our trips into the interior of Australia. The birds live either in pairs or small groups close to the woods. Their song is not unpleasant, but during flight they often let out a rather raw "eek-eek-eek-eek." When sitting alone and without being disturbed, the king parrot may whistle a soft and musical tune that can sound quite enchanting. In the wild they live on seeds, berries, fruit, etc.; sometimes they can be rather destructive to cornfields.

The chances for breeding results are very good, and this, too, has no doubt led to their growing popularity. If we have a roomy aviary we can be sure that our pair will start breeding sooner or later, providing they are left in peace and quiet during the mating and breeding period. I would also advise against housing any other birds in the same aviary, thus allowing the pair every chance for peaceful breeding. The female lays some three to six eggs, measuring 31 x 22.5 mm. Ideal measurements for the nesting box are 35 x 35 cm, with a depth of 90 to 140 cm (14 x 14 x 36-56 inches), which, as you can see, is a very large nesting box. We can either hang up the nesting box or place it against a wall in the aviary. We should place a thick layer about 15-20 cm (6-8 inches) of turf, wood chips, and mulched wood (which can be collected from the hollows of trees) on the bottom of the nesting box. The male will feed the female during the breeding period, and later he will feed the young as well. Ant-eggs, canary nestling food, and universal are highly recommended for the birds during the breeding season. Besides their regular menu (panicum millet, hemp, soaked and broken corn, oats, and grass and weed seeds), they are also very fond of cherries, nuts (shelled), peanuts, juicy apples and pears, peaches, and fresh greens (from willow, beech, and lime trees, as an example). They will very much welcome fresh branches on a daily basis.

Although they may not be at their best in a small aviary, they are elegance personified in a roomy one (for example one that measures ten meters, 31 feet, in length). They may not breed for the first few years, but sooner or later they will raise one or more broods, generously rewarding you for your efforts and expenses on their behalf. This species has a rather strange habit in that many of the females will lay their eggs on the ground in a secluded little corner of the aviary. Nesting boxes that are hung up at a high level and located in the inner part of the aviary will not even be considered by these birds. They will, however, accept as nesting boxes old hollowed-out tree trunks when placed in the outside aviary if they are not hung up too high off the ground. If breeding still does not take place, the birds showing no interest in each other, it would probably be best to switch their partners.

1. Scaly headed parrot, *Pionus maximiliani,* in a cage. This bird is quite common in its native land of southeastern Brazil and Argentina but is seldom imported for captivity; a very desirable bird nonetheless. 2. A nest box for grass parrakeets, *Neophema* species. 3. Pictured here are several types of breeding boxes and feeding cups.

2

3

Cross-breeding results have been achieved with the superb parrot and the red-winged parrot, though I do not feel that these possibilities are to be recommended.

I would like to spend a little time on the green-winged king parrot (*Alisterus chloropterus chloropterus*), which is smaller than the Australian king parrot. Dr. Groen says: "in place of the green wing band, practically the entire wing of the male is a bright light green. The violet area in the neck is also broader, while the red colors are even darker than those of the Australian King Parrot." This species was first discovered in 1878 by Ramsay in the eastern mountain district of Australian New Guinea (now Papua New Guinea). A few are sporadically bred in England; as far as I know, they are not kept in captivity in the United States.

While the Australian king parrot has a cousin (*Alisterus scapularis minor*) that makes his home in the northern regions of Queensland and has brighter coloring, the green-winged king parrot has three cousins: *Alisterus chloropterus moszkowskii* (West Irian, along the Yellow Finch Bay); *Alisterus chloropterus wilhelminae* (West Irian, in the Snowy Mountain region); and *Alisterus chloropterus callopterus* (on the border of West Irian and Papua New Guinea, particularly along the Fly River).

Then there are the species that live on the East Indian islands, for example the Amboina king parrot (*Alisterus amboinensis amboinensis*), obviously from Amboina. This beautiful bird can scarcely be distinguished from the Australian king parrot, except for the fact that it lacks the green marking on the wing. The wings are edged in blue and there is more sky-blue on the back. There is a form of *amboinensis* that lives on Ceram and shows no ornithological difference, which explains why Reichenow classified these birds as one and the same. It has not yet been definitely determined whether Reichenow was correct in doing this; I feel the blue colors on the back and rump are lighter and that this bird's living habits do not exactly parallel those of its Amboinese cousin. However, more intensive studies would be required before this can be ascertained.

Buru Island is the home of yet another bird which Reichenow did definitely see as a different race, namely *Alisterus amboinensis buruensis*. *Alisterus amboinensis dorsalis* lives in West Irian. Both birds have a completely blue back and rump. In addition to a blue back and rump, *Alisterus amboinensis hypophonius* also has blue in the wings. It lives on the Halmahera Islands. *Alisterus amboinensis sulaensis* is an inhabitant of the Sula Islands. This same bird can also be found on Pelang.

GENUS *APROSMICTUS*

The most recent bird classification counts some six species belonging to this genus, of which only one qualifies for description, the very well known and much kept red-winged parrot. This bird lends itself very well to cross-breeding, which is a practice that we, as fanciers, should avoid as much as possible. It is a shame that these birds, which are characterized by their red flight feathers and the broad, short tail, are quite expensive and that it is even a real effort to locate a pair. There are, of course, several good breeders, both domestic and foreign, but the number that is imported is still somewhat limited.

Their build and coloring is much like that of the Australian king parrot, and it will probably remain something of a mystery to many ornithologists as to why this bird was not included in the previous genus. However, since it will not do much good to ponder on the whys and wherefores, we will move onto the details of this lovely bird.

Red-Winged Parrot (*Aprosmictus erythropterus*)

Distribution: Australia: from Kimberly in Western Australia to northern and eastern Australia, to the interior areas of New South Wales, and the northeastern regions of South Australia.

Male: Light green head, neck, and flight feathers. Dark green back, light blue rump, flowing into green-yellow. Green tail, edged in yellow. Light yellow-green underside, or yellow with green glow. Wing-coverts are red. Yellow-green flanks; black 'cloak' feathers. Upper tail-coverts are light greenish brown and yellow-green. Brown eyes; red bill with black band; grayish brown feet.

Female: Green without much gloss. A small amount of red along the edge of the wings. Offspring resemble the female, though the iris is black initially and later red. At one-and-a-half years of age

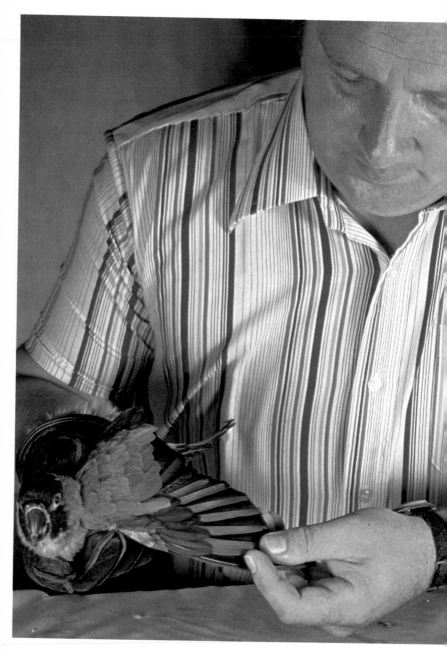

Dr. Vriends with a nanday conure, *Nandayus nenday,* also known as a black-headed conure, points out the blue-marked wings of this attractive bird.

The nanday conure, *Nandayus nenday,* occurs in southeastern Bolivia, southern Mato Grosso, Brazil, Paraguay and northern Argentina.

the males can be distinguished from the females by the black in their feathers.

Length: 34-37 cm (13 3/5-14 4/5 inches); wings 17-20 cm (6 4/5-8 inches); tail 19-22 cm (7 3/5-8 4/5 inches).

Particulars: This bird is definitely at his best in a large aviary. Although quiet by nature, it is nevertheless quite popular. They have a definite preference for germinated seeds. During the breeding time these seeds are even essential, as proved to me in the Netherlands, Australia, and Florida. The female lays some three to six white eggs (32 x 22.5 mm), and she alone sits on them. The male feeds the young birds and defends the nesting box while breeding is taking place.

In the wild, these parrots live in either pairs or small groups, especially in open woods and areas profuse with shrubbery. Their call is not unpleasant to hear. Their flight is beautiful, and when the sun shines on their gorgeous colors it is indeed a lovely sight to behold! They live on seeds, berries, nectar, and the larvae of small insects; in captivity we should include ant-eggs, small mealworms, and enchytrae in their menu. They use tree hollows in which to build their nests. Dr. Groen is mistaken when he says that these birds can be seen by the hundreds in the wild; the largest groups that I saw consisted of eight to fifteen birds.

Ornithologists recognize a subspecies that is smaller in build and is colored with a more intensive red, *Aprosmictus erythropterus coccineopterus*. Then there is the Timor red-winged parrot (*Aprosmictus jonquillaceus*), which, needless to say, lives on Timor; this species is also smaller than the red-winged parrot and has no black in his plumage.

The red-winged parrots are somwhat timid and reserved, and justice is only really done to their beauty when they are housed in a large aviary. The best breeding boxes for these birds are made from old tree trunks. Do not forget that the entrance must have a diameter of at least 8 cm (3 1/5 inches), preferably a little larger. After some 40 days, the young will leave the nest but will still be fed, primarily by the male, for at least another month before they are independent. Once they are independent, it is best to take the young away from their parents.

During the mating and breeding period we should keep a close watch on the male's behavior and attitude because sometimes they become overactive and will do all they can to keep the female in the nesting box, even when there are only unfertilized eggs in the nest or none at all. He may become so aggressive that he may injure the female, and in some instances he may even kill her. If we should get wind of anything like this going on, naturally we must act quickly. This problem can usually be solved by switching partners.

GENUS *PURPUREICEPHALUS*

To the best of my knowledge, this genus consists of only one species. All details can be found in the description of this bird, which follows.

Red-capped Parrot (*Purpureicephalus spurius*)

Distribution: Australia: Southwestern Australia, north to the Moore River and east to Esperance.

Male: The scientific name tells us a few things about this bird: *purpureicephalus*—(Latin: *purpureus*) = purple, (Greek: cephale) = head; *spurius*—(Latin) = false, unreal, incorrect. The cap is a purple-red, as is the neck. The face is grass green. Breast and belly are a purple-blue. Lowest part of underside is red. Green wings with blue flight feathers; yellow-green rump; dark green tail, with outermost feathers being blue. The bill is light blue to horn-colored. Brown eyes, gray feet.

Female: The female is generally as intensive in coloring as the male, except that she does not have the purple-red cap, other than a few brown and red feathers. The purple on the breast and belly is less bright. The shape of her head is rounder, and this is really the only reasonably reliable difference, since some females develop a "red cap" at an older age and are then practically identical to the male in coloring. This notation is also valid with regard to determining the sex of the young, which will not attain adult coloring until after they are twelve months old. The females may get a "red cap" after two or three years, but of course not necessarily.

Length: 32-36 cm (8-9 inches); wings 15-17 cm (6-6 4/5 inches); tail 14-17 cm (5 3/5-6 4/5 inches).

Particulars: As stated under the genus, this is the only species

1

1. Elegant parrot,
Neophema elegans.
This bird, timid in the
wild, becomes a gen-
tle aviary bird willing
to breed freely. 2.
Rear view of an
elegant parrakeet. 3.
Turquoise parrot,
Neophema pulchella.

2

belonging to the genus *Purpureicephalus*. Considering their build and coloring, it would be difficult to place them anywhere else; a separate genus, then, was necessary. Another of the reasons why this species was placed in a genus by itself is the behavior of the male during the mating ritual. It took a great deal of time before man was able to ascertain this behavior, but a few decades ago a group of biologists was successful in learning a little more about the conjugal life of these colorful, though constantly aggressive, Australian broad-tailed birds. This group witnessed the mating dance of the male and saw that it differed from that of other members of the broad-tailed group. While the male dances in tiny paces around the female, he does not swish his tail from left to right and vice versa, but moves the tail in a vertical direction toward the back. Other differences were that while this vertical movement of his beautiful tail was taking place, the head feathers rose, standing up straight, and he made strange scratchy and clucking noises that sounded raw and unpleasant. There are also physical differences, as we already mentioned. To begin with, the beak is hooked; the upper mandible is extremely long and almost completely covers the lower mandible; and the upper mandible has a very long point. As you can see, it makes perfect sense to speak of a new genus here.

In the wild these birds live in small groups or in pairs in the woods and grassy, scrubby plains. In the wild it is easy to spot them due to their raucous calling. They breed in tree hollows, where the female lays five to six eggs from August to November. They feed mainly on the seeds of the eucalyptus trees and on grass and weed seeds. They can do a great deal of damage and are often shot by the farmers. These birds are also very fond of fruit, and woe betide the orchard grower who is visited by a group of red-capped parrots!! Still, it is a shame that these birds are pursued to the extent that they are, because I have been able to determine that their numbers are not as great as often supposed. In fact, I feel that even total extinction is not out of the question if the government takes steps to, for example, poison the water holes (how many other bird species are destroyed by this action as well?), sprinkle poisoned seeds, etc.; it will then only be a matter of a few years before these birds disappear altogether.

Unfortunately, the export ban has been in effect since 1930, with a short interlude in 1953 when the ban was raised temporarily, so that even exports cannot help in preserving this species. Action taken to raise the ban has, up until now, not met with any success. Let us hope that this will soon change, because bird fanciers are more than willing to save this species from extinction. The fanatic bird protection groups, which can also be found in Australia, would do better by giving bird fanciers a helping hand than by burdening them with excessive controls.

In order to maintain the good health of a pair, we should offer the following food: old white bread soaked in honey, sunflower seeds, oats, rye, almonds, shelled peanuts and fruit (pineapple, soft pears, and apples).

Dr. Groen misleadingly states that these birds can be found in the wild in large flocks and that they breed from October to December. The birds lay five to sometimes nine eggs that are brooded by the female from August to November. The male will feed her from his crop on a regular basis. The eggs take 24 days to hatch, and the young leave the nest after about five weeks. Unfortunately these birds remain timid in the aviary, but surely their beautiful colors warrant them being kept more often than they are. Locally bred birds, however, are often quite tame (also quite loud, alas!).

It is also a pity that it is necessary to protect the aviary by affixing metal stripping, because this species has enormous destructive abilities. It goes without saying, no doubt, that the aviary keeper should supply them with fresh branches daily, on which they can work off some of their gnawing desires. Their strong hooked beaks are capable of even biting through sturdy wire! We should, therefore, exercise caution and check on them regularly.

Once they have been acclimatized they can remain outside during the winter months, providing there is ample protection from the elements in the form of a good night shelter. They will usually commence breeding activities in May, and with a little luck we can expect a good brood, especially if we disturb them as little as possible. Cross-breeding has been established with the red-rumped parrot, the western rosella, eastern rosella, and the crimson rosella.

GENUS *LATHAMUS*

This genus consists of just one species, the swift parrot. The

A male king parrakeet, *Alisterus scapularis scapularis,* in his elaborate courtship display.

scientific name has the following meaning: *Lathamus* is Latin for Dr. John Latham (1740-1837), an English ornithologist; *discolor* is Latin for colored differently. The rich variety of colors on an otherwise primarily green plumage has helped lead to this species being placed in a separate genus.

Swift Parrot (*Lathamus discolor*)

Distribution: Australia: Eastern-central Queensland (fairly rare) to Victoria. Southeastern South Australia (they can frequently be found to the west of Adelaide, where I had the opportunity to study them from a short distance) and Tasmania, where they breed.

Male: Green, red forehead and blue cap; sky-blue cheeks and red face. Blue flight feathers and some blue in the tail. The tail is yellow underneath with some red. The wing curve is red and the tail is pointy and shaped like a rake. Central tail feathers are longer than the outer feathers; very long, pointed wings. Brown eyes; horn-colored bill; grayish brown feet.

Female: A little duller in coloring. The young will gain adult coloring after they are six months of age. It is difficult to determine their sex; their colors are not as bright as the male, and they have no red in the under tail-coverts.

Length: 21-23 cm (8 2/5-9 1/5 inches); wings 10-15 cm (4-6 inches); tail 10-15 cm (4-6 inches).

Particulars: These birds live mainly in large groups, even close to man in gardens and parks. I saw them more than once in Hobart in a friend's garden, just a few feet away, while we stood talking quietly in the shade of a tree. They like to live in close proximity of eucalyptus trees and other honey-producing blossoming trees; they also like to eat the insects that are found on flowers and blossoms, as well as petals, seeds, and berries.

These birds live a migratory existence, crossing the Bass Strait to the Australian mainland after the breeding season. Their slender wings enable them to cover this distance quite quickly. During their flight they give voice to a shrill "klink-klink-klink-klink."

The female lays two eggs, sometimes three or four, and selects a tree hollow for the nest. The breeding season depends a great deal on when the eucalyptus trees are in blossom.

These birds are not very frequently kept in captivity. I find this species to be very interesting, however, and most suitable as aviary birds; in fact, their social nature and generally soft voice make them good candidates for a roomy community aviary. Although they will learn to eat seeds, we should offer them plenty of fruit, blossoms in the spring, and fresh twigs and branches the year around.

We have every reason to expect these birds to be a transitional form leaning towards the lories, since their tongue is short and somewhat shaped like a brush.

GENUS *NEOPHEMA*

The representatives of this genus are generally not larger than our finches. The tail is long and the build is slender and elegant. These birds are among the favored by parrot breeders. In general they are typical ground birds; during the cooler hours of the day they seek their food on the ground in the undergrowth and shrubbery. Through the ages they have developed into true wanderers and fast runners, while they keep amazing ornithologists with their climbing abilities in the shrubbery. They are certainly not bad as fliers, and I have seen them in their typical zig-zag pattern flying overhead at such a speed and height that they were just dark specks in the blue sky. In the aviary they are very sweet toward exotic birds. As a result they are often kept in community aviaries where they will also breed without becoming troublesome toward other aviary inhabitants. Their most important seeds are canary seed and millet. Obviously, various grass and weed seeds are always welcome, as are ant-eggs, small mealworms, and whiteworms. Once they have been acclimatized, their constitution is quite strong, though they are sensitive to cold and humidity, so we recommend that they be brought indoors during the fall and winter and placed in a lightly heated area. They are generally pleased with a nesting box that is not hung up too high (1½ meters, 4½ feet), preferably somewhat hidden behind bushes. We should maintain a thick undergrowth because this gives them a feeling of security.

Some authors think that this group is polygamous. I have personally made a close study of these birds for a considerable period

1. Monk parrakeets. 2. Finsch's conures, *Aratinga finschi,* from Central America. 3. Red-fronted conure.

of time and am absolutely certain that this is not the case. In fact, it would not surprise me in the least if they keep the same mate for life!

Scarlet-chested Parrot (*Neophema splendida*)

Distribution: Western portion of New South Wales, northern portion of South Australia, to the coastal areas of the Great Australian Bight, and inward in various colonies in Western Australia.

Male: Head and neck are sea-blue; topside is green; underside is yellow with red crop area. Wings blue-green with bright blue and black. Tail green with yellow and black. Brown eyes; black bill; gray-brown black feet.

Female: Underside is yellow, breast has olive-green shine; darker on back than the male. Sides of head considerably less blue; no red on the crop and chest area.

Length: 21-22 cm (8 1/5-8 4/5 inches); wings 10-11 cm (4-4 2/5 inches); tail 10-11 cm (4-4 2/5 inches).

Particulars: These birds, which are first described by Gould in his famous book on Australian birds published in 1840, are no longer being exported. Fortunately, however, there is a satisfactory number being bred locally each year, although supply has not yet caught up with demand. I have spotted birds that were several miles away from water, and it seems that this is fairly common for them. They seem to be moving more and more inland, and the number living in southwestern Australia keeps increasing, which is a pleasure to report, since their population is not that large to begin with. It is rather strange, and certainly not a favorable point for Australian ornithologists, but this bird went unobserved for over a hundred years; the species was first "rediscovered" in Western Australia in 1941.

Observations reveal this to be a peace-loving bird that likes to keep a low profile. Whenever I approached them, they would hide in the undergrowth and remain so still that I was unable to detect them no matter how hard I tried! The type of terrain they prefer is profuse with various grasses (mulga and spinifex among others), and ordinarily a group of birds will remain in a certain area unless food or water shortages force them to move. They are generally not afraid of man, particularly the birds that live in the vicinity of civilized areas; more than once I observed this species in gardens and public parks. Their soft song is virtually identical to that of the turquoise parrot, except that it is weaker. They do not drink very much; on different occasions I have noticed that birds did not go to water sources for several days! In the aviary, too, they consume very little water, although of course we should give them fresh water daily. In the wild this species uses large cracks and holes in thick branches of low trees (acacia) in which to build their nests. The female lays three, or at the most four to five, eggs. During the breeding period the scarlet-chested parrots stay together in cozy little groups.

In the well-built aviary, with a rain- and draft-free night shelter, this species can spend the winter outdoors as well, providing, of course, they have been acclimated, though I personally feel they are better off indoors in a lightly heated area for the winter months. The female will start breeding quite quickly if we hang a roomy nesting box 20x20, 40 cm deep (8x8x16 inches); entrance hole 5-7 cm (2-3 inches) in the outside section of the aviary. The bottom should be covered with a layer of moist turf and mulch. This same type of nesting box is required for the previous as well as the following species. Half a coconut can be of great service too; the birds will fill the shell with some mulch and pieces of turf.

We should give them the following seeds: canary seed, corn, panicum millet, hemp, oats, sunflower seeds, and grass and weed seeds. They also like the following fruit: apples, pears, soaked raisins, and pineapple. For greens we give them fresh twigs with buds, lettuce, endive, chicory, Brussel sprouts, chickweed, etc.

Immelmann remarks in his book *Die australischer Plattschweif-sittiche*: "A very important observation was made by Y. A. Pepper in Western Australia (correspondence), in his studies of Scarlet Chested Parrots: the females like to use leaves and other soft materials in furnishing their nests. They chewed the leaves from the branches, but did not transport these to their nest in their beak, but instead stuck them under the feathers of their rump. This remarkable manner of transporting nesting materials is also practiced by some Lovebirds (genus *Agapornis*) and a group of small parrots from Africa."

Turquoise Parrot (*Neophema pulchella*)

Distribution: Australia: central Queensland, south through New South Wales (this species has even been known to breed a few times in the vicinity of Sydney) to the border of Victoria.

Male: Sky-blue head, underside yellow-green, becoming lighter toward the tail. Neck, throat, and back are green. Some red in the wings. Blue band on wings and flight feathers. Tail-coverts are green. Outermost tail feathers are yellow; underside of tail is also yellow. Black-brown eyes; black bill; black-brown feet.

Female: No red in the wings; less blue on the head; breast green-yellow underside is a faded yellow, as is the underside of the tail. Young males quickly develop the red in the wings; after eight to ten months they have achieved adult coloring.

Length: 21-22 cm (8 2/5-8 4/5 inches); wings 10-11 cm (4-4 2/5 inches); tail 10-11 cm (4-4 2/5 inches).

Particulars: These birds, which live in pairs or small groups in grasslands and open woods, spend a lot of time on the ground searching for seeds and are typical "dusk" birds. They were first discovered in 1788 and in 1792 were extensively described by Shaw. In that time, as in the two years that John Gould travelled through Australia (1839-40), this species was often seen. During my stay in Australia, I only saw them once or twice; in eastern Australia, however, they are fairly common, so that at least we need not worry about their extinction at the present time. It is difficult to predict how the population of this species will develop, but it would certainly not surprise me if there were more in captivity than in the wild, thanks to the determination of thousands of aviculturists who realize that this beautiful species is slowly but surely becoming extinct.

Early in the spring the female will start to inspect the nesting boxes 20 x 20, 40 cm depth (8 x 8 x 16 inches); entrance hole 6 cm (2 2/5 inches) in diameter, and if we place moist turf, woodchips, and the like inside the box, she will soon start to expand her family. She usually lays four to seven white eggs, sometimes eight (23-24 x 16-18 mm). After a good twenty days the chicks hatch, and the male will then become active in bringing food for his offspring. Before that, his only role in the breeding process was feeding his wife. Soon the female will help with the feeding of the young ones. During the breeding cycle, all *Neophema* species should be offered stale white bread soaked in milk or water, germinated seeds, a normal seed menu, and a rich variety of greens and fresh branches with buds. Only specimens that have been locally bred should be kept outdoors during the winter. Imported birds (including those from Japan) are generally not as strong and require being kept indoors in a lightly heated area for the first twelve months.

Two clutches per year is not at all unusual; in the wild they usually breed three times. The aviary must be roomy and certainly not damp, because dampness is very dangerous for these small, beautiful birds. For the sake of our birds (and who would want to take chances and experiment with expensive species?) it is wise to remove the nesting boxes after the young of the second clutch have flown out and in this way force both the fledglings and parents to spend the night in the night shelter. Since the molting period of the young birds takes place during the winter months, it may be advisable to have them spend the first few winters indoors; once they are a little older and accustomed to climate and aviary life, they should be able to get through the winter molting period without any problem.

Turquoise parrots are not tolerant toward fellow species during the breeding season and must not be kept in the same aviary. Even when the young have flown out and become independent, the male often follows them in an aggressive manner so that it is best to separate the young from their parents. This aggressive pursuit by the father is only directed at the young males; the female chicks have nothing to worry about! The father may even start this pursuit before the young are completely independent. It is important, therefore, that we keep an eye out for this type of thing. Should this situation develop, it will become necessary for us to separate the young males and feed them by hand. I have personally separated the young males and placed them in an adjacent aviary so that the father (and the mother of course) could feed them through the wire. Another possibility is to place the young in a reasonably sized cage in the aviary; the parents will then feed them through the bars, so we will not have the problem of rearing them ourselves. After two weeks the fledglings become independent, so we will then no longer need to concern ourselves with this problem. Since the young birds are quite wild and nervous, it is impor-

3

4

5

1. Superb parrot (left) and budgerigar (right). 2. Canary-winged parrakeets. 3. Jandaya conure. 4. Peach-fronted conure. 5. White-eared conure.

tant that we place plants, branches, or twigs on the roof and sides of the aviary to help warn the young birds of the obstacles (especially the wire). After about a week we can remove these twigs gradually, because the young birds will have become accustomed to the layout of the aviary by then.

I would certainly advise you to make nest inspections, because there is always the possibility that the female may have laid a new batch of eggs while she still has a clutch of dependent chicks in her nest. This is why we should provide our birds with more than one nesting box, so that she does not have to use the same nest in which to lay her eggs. Nevertheless, this is not necessarily the only solution, because sometimes the female prefers the old nest anyway and simply deposits her eggs between her little sprouts!

Elegant Parrot (*Neophema elegans*)

Distribution: Southern portion of New South Wales, western Victoria, South Australia (north to Flinders Ranges) and southwestern Australia (north to Moora and east to Esperance).

Male: Golden yellow; lighter on the underside of the tail. Yellow triangle between bill and eyes. Small blue eyebrow. Blue edges on the wing feathers. Some orange feathers on the lower belly. Olivegreen back. Black flight feathers.

Female: Less vivid yellow; no orange feathers on the belly (although some females may have these; they usually disappear, however, after one or two molts). Blue flight feathers. Young males are a brighter yellow than the females at the time they leave the nest, but do not yet have the band on the forehead. After six months the juvenile molting is finished.

Particulars: This species, which lives in pairs or in small groups, is considered one of the most common of the *Neophema* representatives. They can often be found not too far away from civilization and have even been found on the northern border of Western Australia, in the Pilbara District, which is in the tropics! They live near woods, though not in them, on open grass terrain and new plantations; it would almost seem as if they avoid trees. Many of them live along the coast, where we saw them several times early in the morning, flying high up in the sky.

The southern areas of Australia are home to the subspecies *Neo-*

phema elegans carteri, which is less vivid in coloring, though only professional ornithologists encumber themselves with the slight differences.

In Australia this bird is also referred to as the elegant grass parrot because it lives mainly on the seeds of grass and other plants. He is a migratory bird and can be found in cultivated areas where clover is grown, such as in southwestern Australia. The female lays four to five white eggs (17 x 20 mm); in the wild a couple only rears one clutch per season, generally in August to October. The care required by these birds parallels that of the prior species. The first specimens were brought to Europe—the London Zoo to be precise—in 1862 and rapidly became popular because of their easy care and breeding. Various cross-breeding results have been achieved, mainly with the turquoise, scarlet-chested, and blue-winged parrots. To ensure good breeding results it is wise to provide them with deep nesting boxes about 40 cm (16 inches) and to cover the bottom with moist leaves and turf.

Rock Parrot (*Neophema petrophila*)

Distribution: Along the coast and the island of southwestern and southern Australia, from Shark Bay to the southeastern point of South Australia. Immelmann notes that there is an interruption in the territory of the rock parrot that is located somewhere along the coast of the Great Australian Bight at the western border of South Australia. It is at this point that the Nullarbar Desert has claimed more area and is now in the immediate vicinity of the coastal region; the sand stretches do not offer the rock parrot even a meager existence. The exact length of this break in the rock parrot's territory is not known.

Male and female: The coloring of the rock parrot is much like that of the elegant parrot, with a few obvious differences: there is quite a lot more green on the head and more blue in the wings. They are also a little larger, and their build is not as slender. The darker colors seem to occur a lot with birds that live on islands. The eyes are brown; the beak is bluish black; the feet are brownish gray.

Length: 23-24 cm (9 1/5-9 3/5 inches); wings 11-12 cm (4 2/5-4 4/5 inches); tail 11-12 cm (4 2/5-4 4/5 inches).

Particulars: The scientific name tells us something about the natural habitat of this bird: *petros* is Greek for rock, and *philos* is also Greek and boils down to "being keen on," "liking a lot." They do, then, certainly like to live among the rocks and in heather and sand-dune country that often is devoid of trees and bushes. They will even lay their four or five eggs in a hole among the rocks.

Somewhat sturdier of build and with orange on the belly is the orange-bellied parrot (*Neophema chrysogaster*). This species has more green in his plumage and more yellow in his tail. The scientific name comes from the Greek *chrysos* meaning gold, and *gaster* meaning belly. They live along the coast of South Australia, Victoria, and the south of New South Wales; they can also be found on Tasmania. The look a lot like the blue-winged parrot, but their menu is quite different. Their lifestyle is also similar to that of the blue-winged parrot. Unfortunately their numbers seem to be steadily decreasing; in fact, during the last five years there have been no breeding results registered on Tasmania! To quote Immelmann on this subject:

"The Orange-Bellied Parrot has even become very rare on the Australian mainland. An individual lost specimen flew into the immediate vicinity of Melbourne in 1950. The Orange-Bellied Parrot can still be regularly found on the small, mostly uninhabited islands of the Bass Strait. In the coastal areas of New South Wales their appearances have also generally been in the form of individual birds. Noteworthy is their mass appearance during the 1890's. At that time they appeared in such large numbers that shooting contests were organized, with this species as the target! Their origin has remained unknown. In light of the fact that the Orange-Bellied Parrot is the bird least kept in captivity of the *Neophema* representatives, it has been absolutely ruled out that these individual appearances could have been escaped specimens. It is very likely that a tremendous overpopulation developed in a certain region, forcing part of the population to move to different territory. Such a phenomenon is not all that rare in the Australian bird world. Under particularly favorable circumstances, such as may occur as a result of an overabundant rainfall, many species breed several times, one right after the other, so that an over-population is soon developed. When the food sources decrease, and there is insufficient supply left, a part of the population will have to move elsewhere." *(Die australischen Plattschweifsittiche.)*

Blue-winged Parrot (*Neophema chrysostoma*)

Distribution: Western part of New South Wales and Victoria, southern part of South Australia, King Island, and Tasmania.

Male: Green. Darker on the back and shoulders. Bright green-yellow toward the belly. Lores orange-yellow. Blue wings. Inner-most tail feathers are vivid orange-yellow. Blue band across the forehead continues to the eye (in the elegant parrot this band continues to the other side of the eye). Many males have an orange-pink marking on the belly.

Female: Generally less vivid in coloring; she has a yellow-green glow woven through the blue. Smaller band on the forehead. Flight feathers are brown (black in the male). Brown eyes; blue-gray bill; brown-gray feet. Young birds do not develop the fore-head band until later, though some have a vague outline of one. The blue in the wings is usually not as sharp. It will take a full year for the young birds to achieve adult coloring.

Length: 22-23 cm (8 4/5-9 1/5 inches); wings 10-11 cm (4-4 2/5 inches); tail 10-11 cm (4-4 2/5 inches).

Particulars: This gorgeous bird, which inhabits all types of ter-rain, is very common in Australia and a very lovely and frequent choice of aviary keepers in Europe. There are quite a number of them in Tasmania as well, even in the winter, though a good many fly to the mainland for this season. Their way of life greatly parallels that of the elegant parrot, although they are not as popular among aviculturists as the elegant parrot, possibly because of their somewhat plumper build. European-bred speci-mens are generally quite healthy and can be tamed very quickly, even to the point where they will take a treat out of their keeper's hand. This bird is also very suitable for a community aviary. I have had good breeding results from a couple that was housed in a large aviary together with a couple of cockatiels, various types of weaver couples, a pair of cardinals, and three pairs of budgerigars. A strange combination, I will gladly admit . . .

1

2

3

4

5

1. Patagonian conure.
2. Tui parrakeet. 3.
Orange-fronted con-
ure. 4. Tovi or beebee
parrakeet. 5. Rose-
ringed parrakeet.

As already said, a couple will readily breed. The female lays five to seven eggs (18 x 23 mm). In the wild some of them live in fairly large groups, and even during the breeding period a certain amount of community lifestyle remains; I have observed them in groups of ten to fifteen pairs during this period. On several occasions I have seen more than one nest close together in the same tree; they use holes and such in trees in which to build their nests. I have also seen them in the company of swift parrots and green rosellas. Eight times my wife and I found the nest of a blue-winged parrot in the old nests of owls and once or twice in the nests of starlings and swallows. The average height of these nests was between five and thirty meters (15-90 feet), usually as high as possible.

In captivity these birds love sweet, not very hard apples, which is rather strange since, as far as I know, they are not very keen on fruit in the wild and feed mainly on grass and weed seeds. In the aviary, and particularly during the breeding season, we should not omit stale white bread soaked in water; the same applies to canary seed, panicum millet, a small amount of hemp, oats, corn, and small or cracked sunflower seeds. Experience has shown that it would be a mistake to give them nesting boxes that are too small. They should measure at least 20 x 20 cm, and 40 cm deep (8 x 8 x 16 inches); entrance hole diameter 5-7 cm (2-3 inches). The nesting boxes should be hung up in the outside section of the aviary. Underneath the entrance opening we should affix a piece of wire or, better still, a piece of bark or cork because the female has the habit of spending quite some time leaning against the box with her head in front of the nest opening.

Finally, I would like to point out that this bird can be crossed with the elegant, turquoise, and rock parrots. Its scientific name is somewhat strange, since it is made up of two Greek words: *chrysos*, meaning gold, and *stoma*, meaning bill. Only with a certain kind of lighting does the bluish gray bill give the appearance of being gold.

GENUS *PSEPHOTUS*
This genus is basically made up of three groups, *Psephotus*, *Psephotellus*, and *Northiella*, that could be seen as separate genera.

The Greek *Psephotus* means "inlaid with small stones," such as mosaic. All these birds, which are definitely inhabitants of dry climate zones, are primarily seed-eaters, though they seldom eat grain varieties, and as such, are not considered destructive by farmers. They will rarely visit fruit orchards or other plantations.

Various representatives of this genus are successfully kept and bred by fanciers. They have become increasingly popular during the last few years, although very few birds arrive from overseas (mostly through the black market); local breeding results are more than satisfactory, though of course demand is still greater than supply. Various representatives must be placed in an aviary by themselves, because otherwise they will constantly attack other aviary inhabitants, injuring or even killing them. Even fellow species and larger parrot types are subject to their aggression and may well become seriously injured. Personally, I even prefer to place them in a free-standing aviary rather than one that is separated by wire into various compartments, because some of the birds belonging to this genus will not rest until they have made their way into the next compartment, at the expense of woodwork and wire, where they can give free reign to their aggressive and destructive nature! Caution is definitely a watchword here.

Paradise Parrot (*Psephotus pulcherrimus*)

Distribution: Australia: Queensland and the most northern and northeastern parts of New South Wales.

Male: Bright red forehead, black crown. Yellow-green face. Green shoulders; wing-coverts bright red. Back and wings chocolate brown. Sky-blue belly, changing to red; under tail-coverts are red. Purple-blue rump. Central tail feathers green; outermost tail feathers blue. Black-brown eyes; green-yellow bill with black tip; light brown feet.

Female: Yellow band on the forehead, brown crown. Face and throat whitish yellow. The red in her plumage is less vivid than in that of the male. Breast is light green-yellow, changing to off-white at the under tail-coverts. Sky-blue rump. The brown in the back and wings is a little less sharp. She has a round head that is generally larger in build than that of the male.

Length: 30-31½ cm (12-12 3/5 inches); wings 13-15 cm (5 1/5-6 inches); tail 15-17 cm (6-6 4/5 inches).

Particulars: This bird is extremely rare and many people suppose it has become extinct. I never saw any trace of this species during my expeditions and travels. The species was first seen in 1844 by John Gilbert in Darling Downs. Gould described the bird a year later in England, basing his description on a skin that was sent to him. Until the turn of the century this bird was relatively common; after 1900, however, it was thought to have become extinct. From 1918 to 1927 a few specimens were spotted in Queensland and in northern New South Wales, but since 1927 there has been no further trace of them. Yet it is not certain whether or not this bird is definitely extinct. Immelman correctly makes the following comments:

"When one considers that the natural habitat of this species lies in the least populated regions of Australia, the possibility should not be ruled out that small groups of these birds have managed to survive without having been seen by man. There are certain cases in the history of Australian ornithology where certain species were considered extinct for many years, only to suddenly appear in large numbers, apparently out of nowhere. A definite statement with regard to the existence of the Paradise Parrot is not yet possible at the present time."

The female lays her three to four white eggs (24 x 20 mm) in termite mounds. She will hollow out one of the rooms in the termite hill with her beak so there is enough room for her eggs and later the fledglings. Some nests have been found on the banks of little creeks. It is understandable, therefore, that this species often fell victim to snakes and even larger fish. An older Australian ornithologist once told me how he had witnessed a snook grab a young parrot that was crawling out of its nest and swim away with it.

Let us hope that this colorful parrot is not extinct and soon shows itself again, because it certainly is beautification in an otherwise rather isolated and dead-looking landscape.

Golden-shouldered Parrot (*Psephotus chrysopterygius* or *Psephotellus chrysopterygius*)

Distribution: Australia: Cape York Peninsula, from somewhere near the Watson River (west) to the region around Laura (east) (per Cayley). In other words, along the coast of the Carpentaria Gulf (northwestern Queensland). There are two subspecies, *Psephotus chrysopterygius chrysopterygius* from the northern region of Queensland and *Psephotus chrysopterygius dissimilis* from the Northern Territories (the so-called hooded parrot, discussed separately).

Male: Black brown crown; yellow forehead; green gray cheeks. Underside and flanks bluish-gray with green shine. Part of the belly feathers and the under-tail-coverts are red. Shoulders and back light brownish-green. Lower back and rump greenish-black, as are the upper tail feathers which are margined in white. Small flight feathers are blue. Primaries bluish black with light edges. Secondary wing coverts golden-yellow. Brown eyes, blue-yellow bill; brownish-gray feet.

Female: Light green on the back. Rump greenish-blue (Note: most males also have a bluish-green rump, though many birds in the wild have a black reflection, or greenish-black rump feathers). No yellow in the wings. All markings are less defined; she lacks the black "cap."

Length: 23-24 cm (9 1/5-9 3/5 inches); wings 10-11 cm (4-4 2/5 inches); tail 13-14 cm (5-6 inches).

Particulars: The Golden Shouldered Parrots live in pairs during the breeding period. They are excellent fliers, and their flight pattern is 'wavy.' In the wild they are extremely alert birds, taking wing for the least provocation. Around the water-holes they are constantly on the look-out for danger. More than once I have observed them close to a water source, looking around for forty-five minutes or longer, finally making a hasty trip to the water's edge, drining some water quickly, and returning again to their look-out. Their main source of food is insects and all sorts of grass and weed seeds. Outside of the breeding period, they live together in small groups. They build their nests in termite hills; the so-called hooded parrot, on the other hand, sometimes uses tree cavities in which to build the nest.

The female lays four to six white eggs (20.6 x 17.7 mm). It is quite remarkable that a moth-like insect (*Neossiosynoeca scatophaga*) always lays her eggs in the immediate proximity of the nest cavity of a golden-shouldered parrot. The larvae feed on the drop-

1

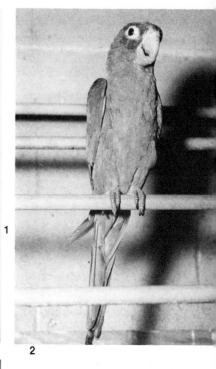

2

3

1. Bronze-winged parrot. 2.
Red-masked conure. 3.
Lutino Indian ringneck
parrakeet. 4. Moustached
parrakeet. 5. Malabar
parrakeet. 6. Scaly-headed
parrot. 7. Canary-winged
parrakeet.

pings of the fledglings, and, as Cayley says, ". . . they keep clean the floor, and the feet of the young." This "living together" is called symbiosis. Breeding results are very difficult to achieve in captivity, which explains why even in Australia not many fanciers keep this species; they must be housed separately during the breeding season because they are quite aggressive and will cause problems for other breeding birds.

They were imported to London in 1897 and soon after were also kept in a Berlin zoo. This species is not as popular as the hooded parrot, which is certainly not an unknown variety to many breeders and can generally be purchased through advertisements in bird magazines. Both *Psephotus c. chrysopterygius* and *Psephotus chrysopterygius dissimilis* are sensitive to cold temperatures and should, therefore, be placed in a lightly heated area during the fall and winter. This is not to imply that they are difficult to keep; most of the details for their care run parallel with those that apply to the other *Psephotus* representatives.

Hooded parrot (*Psephotus chrysopterygius dissimilis*)

Distribution: Northern Territories, Australia.

Male: Black crown; blue-gray cheeks. Brown-black back and wings. Underside is green-blue to blue-gray. Under tail-coverts are pink. Tail is green, changing to black toward the underside. The underside of the tail has some light blue feathers. Secondary coverts are brown-black; the balance of the wing is deep yellow. Flight feathers brownish black. Gray bill; dark brown eyes; flesh-colored feet.

Female: Light green; underside and rump are light blue. No yellow in the wings. Young males lack the black on the head. The young do not achieve adult coloring until they are two years of age.

Particulars: These birds, which were discovered by Prof. Dr. K. Dahl (Arnhemsland) in 1894, live in small groups or in pairs in open wooded country, especially where an Australian grass known scientifically as *Triodia irritans* grows. Although they usually use termite hills in the wild, reasonable breeding results can be obtained in captivity in nesting boxes. It is not always easy to encourage them to breed, however, because their molting period coincides with the breeding season. Dr. Groen from Holland and Dr. Burkard from Switzerland, however, seem to manage success every so often, while Mr. Benvie from Scotland, according to Mr. Van der Mark, already possesses some 22 specimens and has fledglings being reared during the Christmas season. Mr. Van der Mark says further that: "Some pairs breed in our spring time, as used to be the case with Dr. Polak of Amersfoort (Netherlands), and with the professional breeder Boosey from England, so that we can see this beautiful parrot species definitely has a future with breeders, although fresh imports would seem necessary." Red-rumped parrots can serve as foster parents, should this be necessary. Cross-breeding is possible with the golden-shoulder parrot, the red-rumped parrot, the mulga parrot, and with the paradise parrot. Some cross-breeding is compelled by necessity, too, because in 1965 Europe only had 20 unrelated breeding pairs and a few unrelated specimens.

Dr. R. Burkard from Switzerland, who is director of a large concern there, is a bird fancier in a class all his own; there are few in the world of his genre. His fantastic aviaries on the factory complex just outside of Zurich often boast some of the rarest exotic bird species, caught by his own private bird catcher. In 1962, he bought from the well known fancier Melides a pair of hooded parrots at least five years of age and in moderate health. They were housed in a cold cage about 60 cm (24 inches) long . . . not exactly ideally housed! Dr. Burkard gave this pair the very best of care, and in the fall of 1964 they showed signs that indicated an interest to breed. Four young were hatched, but Dr. Burkard did not see them until they were taken out of the nesting box in a state of malnutrition. In December 1964, the pair started a second clutch, and of the four eggs that were laid two hatched, apparently the first and the fourth since the one bird was quite a bit larger than the other when seen during the nest inspection. The larger one left the nest ten days later! Fortunately the female continued to feed the smaller chick even after the first one had left the nest.

After a thorough molting during the spring and summer, the same pair bred again in August 1965: four eggs, four young. The second clutch produced three eggs and three young in October. Although Dr. Burkard already considered these to be tremendous breeding results, the male started feeding and courting the female again shortly after the last young had left the nest! In December there were another five eggs in the box, and in January 1966 all eggs were hatched; the young birds grew up healthy and strong!

Of the three varieties of nesting boxes that were offered, namely the rosella box, a 40 cm (16 inches) high small vertical box, and a lovebird type box with an inspection door in the side, the last one was chosen, though the five young hooded parrots must have been a little cramped! A mixture of turf, mulched wood, and planing chips covered the bottom in a layer about 2 cm (4/5 inches) thick. The breeding time took about 18-19 days, and the young left the nest after about 4½ weeks. The young can fly well immediately, but have a little trouble in accurately landing on the perches, so Dr. Burkard covered the walls of the aviary with pine branches. Although the young continued to be fed by the parents for at least two weeks after leaving the nest, they started searching for food from the first day that they flew out. Externally the young resemble the female, but the under tail-coverts are not yet a bright red, while the beak is yellow and not yet flesh-colored.

Dr. Burkard's breeding pair are housed in his "finch house," where they have an inside aviary of 3 meters squared (about 85 sq. feet) and a flight of the same dimensions. The inside aviary is heated in the winter to 18° C. (65° F.), although 10-12° C. (50-52° F.) would be sufficient for the breeding of these birds. An automatic light timer achieves longer days for them, which start at 4:30 a.m.

Outside the breeding period, hooded parrots are given panicum millet varieties, a small amount of sunflower seeds, and greens. During the breeding period they are given soft food and sprouted sunflower seeds (especially the striped variety and, in smaller amounts, the white type). They also very much enjoy green blades of grass.

Mulga Parrot (*Psephotus varius*)

Distribution: Central Australia from southwestern Queensland to the center of New South Wales, as well as the northwest of Victoria, the center of South Australia, and to deep into Western Australia.

Male: Green belly and breast, lightening to blue on the head.

344

Yellow band across the forehead; yellow under tail-coverts. Obvious yellow shoulder marking, sometimes interspersed with orange feathers. Green rump has two horizontal bands, the top one light green, the lower one deep red. Wing curves and tail are blue. I would like to point out, however, that there are many color variations within this species, as indicated by their scientific name. The red, in particular, seems to show itself in many varieties, which explains why this bird was originally divided into several races. Gray bill; dark brown eyes; pink feet.

Female: Brownish green with light green under tail-coverts. The belly is also light green. Bright red shoulder marking. The forehead band is barely discernible. The birds soon resemble the parents, and there should be no difficulty in sexing them shortly after they fly out of the nest. Young males are considerably greener in color.

Length: 25 cm (10 inches); wings 10-11 cm (4-4 2/5 inches); tail 14-15 cm (5 3/5-6 inches).

Particulars: This bird, first discovered in 1820, is very popular lately and is regularly offered for reasonable prices in bird magazines. In the wild they seem to prefer rather barren areas, although there also seems to be a tendency to follow man and his culture. They are often seen in the company of red-rumped parrots, which have a similar lifestyle, and spend a great deal of time on the ground. On rare occasions I have seen them peacefully together with the so-called twenty-eight parrot (*Barnardius zonarius semitorquatus*). They feed on grass and weed seeds, fruits, berries (*Loranthus murrayi,* as an example), charcoal, larvae, gall wasps, etc. The reasoning behind the consumption of charcoal is not known (see *Agricultural Magazine,* 1964, Forshaw).

This species breeds in the hollows of thick branches, preferably in eucalyptus trees. The female lays four to six eggs (18-20 x 22-23 mm). After 21 days the eggs are hatched. Both parents feed their young, which leave the nest after five weeks, although the parents will continue to feed them for a few more weeks. In the wild the young stay with their parents much longer and generally they will separate when the next breeding cycle approaches after about one year. One should keep in mind that recently imported birds are very delicate and need to be banded with the utmost of care. They should not be placed in the outside aviary for some time, but

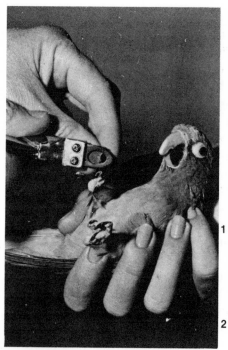

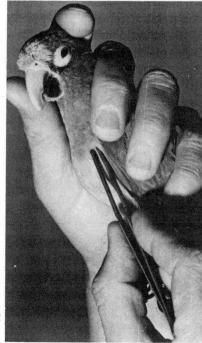

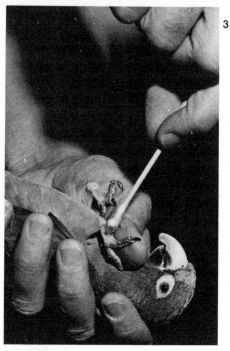

1. Toenail clipping. Be careful not to cut into a vein. 2. Ingrown feathers should be pulled out as illustrated above. 3. Antiseptic is being applied to a cut on this bird's foot. 4 & 5. This halfmoon's beak is overgrown and needs trimming. 6. Administering medicine with a plastic dropper. 7. Your bird must be thoroughly dried to protect it against chills after a bath given in the winter.

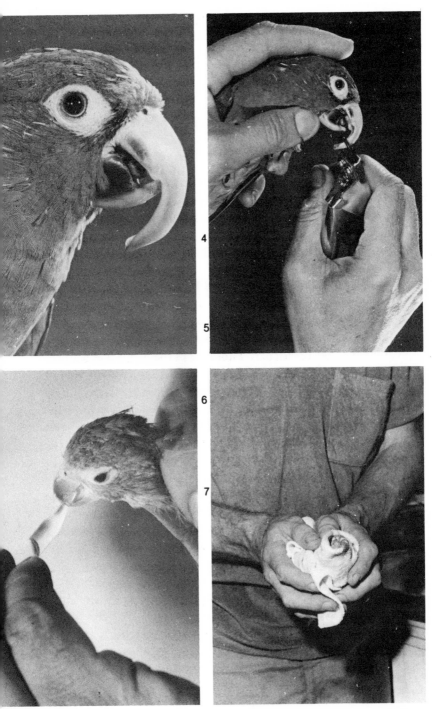

4

5

6

7

should first become totally accustomed to room temperature. It is understandable that once they are outside they be brought indoors for the fall and winter and placed in a light and airy area.

The first breeding results in captivity were obtained in France in 1877. Cross-breeding can occur with the red-rumped, golden-shouldered, and blue bonnet parrots (Forshaw). This bird is an ideal choice for the specialized breeder, offering many possibilities.

Blue Bonnet Parrot (*Psephotus haematogaster*)

Distribution: Southwestern Queensland, New South Wales to northwestern Victoria, as well as the northeastern and southern parts of South Australia and the southern regions of Western Australia. There are several subspecies. Immelman says the following about the blue bonnet:

"The Blue Bonnet Parrot has been repeatedly placed in a separate genus—*Northiella* Mathews—which leads from the actual *Psephotus* species to the Rosellas (*Platycercus* genus) and the Port Lincoln Parrot (*Barnardius* genus)—per Condon and von Boetticher. This split in the genus was adopted because of the shape of the wing and the structure of the five outer-most flight feathers. Recently, however, Cain pointed out that this division cannot be continued. Apart from the fact that a new genus should not be established on the basis of just one not so important morphological trademark, the form of the wing and flight feathers points to various signs of an adaptive nature, which can differ greatly even with closely related species (e.g. *Vini josefinae* and *Vini papous* in the *Trichoglossini*). This difference, then, is not an appropriate base on which to make classification changes. Therefore, I choose to follow Cain's suggestion, and prefer to leave the Blue Bonnet Parrot classified in the *Psephotus* genus."

We recognize four geographical races:

1. *Psephotus haematogaster haematogaster* lives in the dry interior of South Australia, western New South Wales, and southern Queensland. Mostly grayish brown on breast, back, and back of the head. Face, wing edges, and tail are blue; belly is yellow with red; red flanks; under tail-coverts are deep yellow. The red in the female is less vivid.

2. *Psephotus haematogaster haematorrhous,* known as the red-vented blue bonnet, lives in slightly less dry areas near the slopes of the mountain ranges in eastern Australia, to the east of the territory of the previous race. It is not found as far south and limits its natural distribution to New South Wales and southern Queensland (Immelmann). The difference between this subspecies and the previous one is the deep red of the feathers under the tail.

3. *Psephotus haematogaster pallescens* lives in the vicinity of Lake Eyre and Lake Frome in South Australia. Their habitat is dry and rather barren, much resembling a desert landscape. Immelman correctly refers to this bird as a desert race. All colors are considerably paler, so this subspecies can easily be distinguished from the other races.

4. *Psephotus haematogaster narethae,* sometimes called the Naretha parrot. This name is derived from Naretha, an unimportant settlement along the transcontinental railway where this race was first observed. This race, then, is an inhabitant of Western Australia west of the Nullarbor Desert. Immelman says of this subspecies: "This race is divided by a good 600 kilometers of waterless desert from all the other subspecies of Blue Bonnet Parrots. Currently, his terrain covers an area of just 35x290 kilometers. It is quite likely that this terrain was a great deal larger in former days, but the progressive drying out of the continent has pushed him back more and more." This race is quite a bit smaller than the others and the coloring is more intense and deeper. This race used to be considered a separate species because of the enormous gap between its territory and that of the other races and because its consequent behavior is markedly different.

Particulars: As we have already seen, the blue bonnet parrot is a typical representative of the savannahs where there are few trees but here and there some low shrubs. Research has shown that their numbers are slowly decreasing. I have observed on a few occasions that certain pairs in the wild completely skipped over a breeding season without there being any obvious reason for this! It is of course a fact that a lot of savannah terrain is being converted to cultivated fields and grazing land, with natural shrubbery being destroyed (the birds eat the seeds). As far as living habits are concerned, the blue bonnet resembles the other species of the genus. They prefer to live in pairs, though some live in small groups except during the breeding season, and seek their food, which is mainly seeds, on the ground. The mating dance of the male is well worth seeing: he stretches himself as high as possible, vibrates his raised wings, makes rapid nodding movements with his head, and turns his spread-out tail to and fro. In contrast with most of the other broad-tailed varieties, his forehead feathers stick out at that time (Immelmann). Both male and female conduct an intensive search, sometimes taking days, for a suitable nesting place. They generally will choose a hollow in thick branches or in the trunks of trees, including dead trees. The female lays four to seven eggs (18x22 mm) on which she alone will sit. The male feeds her from the crop during this process. They can certainly be considered steadfast in staying on the eggs, because we have gotten as close as less than a meter from the nest before the female took wing and on a curving course called sharply, making a sound much like that of the rosellas. The young will leave the nest at one month, though both parents will continue to feed them for quite some time. Even when they have become independent, the young still like to stay with their parents for a little longer.

The care of these birds runs parallel to that of the previous species. Experience has shown that the first two races are the most popular with fanciers, although they are just as aggressive as the others and can only be bred working with a pair in a fairly roomy aviary by themselves. They also tend to be quite noisy, which makes them less than ideal for keeping in a suburban or urban area—if you would prefer to stay on good terms with your neighbors! The blue bonnet was first imported into Europe (England) in 1862 and bred for the first time in the London Zoo some twenty years later. Young birds will achieve adult coloring after about seven months.

Red-rumped Parrot (*Psephotus haematonotus*)

Distribution: Australia: Southwestern Queensland to close to the coast of Victoria and the south and northeast of South Australia. This species is sometimes known as the red-backed parrot, grass parrot, and ground parrot. (The last name, in particular, can be confusing, because this name is also sometimes used to designate the paradise parrot and *Pezoporus wallicus,* which is a parimarily green bird with yellow scalloped markings over the entire body and a red band on the forehead. That bird looks a lot like the night parrot (*Geopsittacus occidentalis*) which is smaller and has no red coloring; the cheeks are yellow with a green reflective glow. Both birds have virtually never been imported into Europe; in 1867-1868 the night parrot was kept in a London Zoo for study purposes, but died after two months. This bird is very rare in Australia, and in some areas it is believed to have become extinct.)

Male: Green; yellow flanks and belly. Vivid red back. Flight feathers black-blue. Blue-green tail, banded in white. Brown eyes; grayish black bill; grayish brown feet.

Female: Considerably duller in coloring. She has a lot more yellow in her plumage, though she lacks the bright yellow in the wings and the red of the back. Belly and wing feathers are edged in black. A few blue feathers along the curve of the wing. Young birds can be readily sexed, since the males are a brighter green on the head and already display a vague red on the back and rump. Sometimes, however, the young females may have some red on the back and rump as well.

Length: 26-27.5 cm (10 2/5-11 inches); wings 12-13 cm (4 4/5-5 1/5 inches); tail 13.8-14.3 cm (5 3/5-5 4/5 inches).

Particulars: These birds are certainly not unknown to aviculturists and are regularly offered for sale in bird magazines. Even beginners can confidently start with a pair of red-rumped parrots. They are very sweet, even toward other birds, though they like to give fellow species 'a big mouth.' They are quite common in Australia, both in pairs and in large groups (sometimes about 150 birds), and we can approach them quite closely—at least this has been my experience. Sometimes they can be seen sitting in long rows on the barren rocks, singing to each other! Their song is something like that of the thrush; both male and female sing. They seem to have a preference for the grasslands, where they are usually on the ground.

The female lays four to seven white eggs (22 x 19.2 mm) in a tree hollow and will sit on them for 25 days. When the young are a good month old they will leave the nest, but will still be fed for quite some time by both parents. We should give them a roomy nesting box that measures at least 25 x 12 x 35 cm (10 x 5 x 14 inches); entrance opening diameter 6 cm (2 2/5 inches). Independent birds should be separated from the parents because the male will chase and possibly injure them.

In 1858 the first specimens arrived in England and were successfully bred, particularly in the London Zoo. The first breeding successes in Holland date from 1865. Experience has shown that although red-rumped parrots are good natured toward other birds, as mentioned above, they will not tolerate fellow species in the same aviary. I have always had the most success with housing a pair by themselves in a roomy aviary. If we offer them enough nesting opportunities, we should have no trouble in breeding these birds. One should not be too surprised though, if there is a considerable gap between the hatching of the first and last eggs. Constant attention, the proper food, and peace and quiet are essential if we are to achieve good breeding results. My personal preference is to place the birds in an aviary that is at least 5 meters long and 2 meters wide (15 x 6 feet). A community aviary (one with a few exotic birds) is ideal. Two or three clutches per year are not rare. They may stay outside during the winter months providing, of course, they have a well built night shelter that affords them protection from the elements. We must pay special attention to one point, and that is the floor. This must be kept immaculately clean, since they seek all their food on the ground; spoiled food that is picked up by them can easily lead to disease. Red-rumped parrots very much enjoy sprouted grass seeds.

To avoid egg binding, particularly with young birds, we should not hang up the nesting boxes until the end of March or beginning of April. This species makes excellent foster parents for other parrot and parrakeet varieties. In England in 1935 mutations were bred, and since then yellow red-rumped parrots have been bred all over the world; they are particularly popular in Europe and the U.S.

Van der Mark says this about the yellow mutation:

"The birds that were bred consisted of a lovely yellow female and a not so beautiful male, but the female was mated with a regular Red Rumped Parrot and this union produced beautiful yellow birds of both sexes. Which combination constitutes the best mating remains to be seen; establishing this is made even more difficult because a heterozygous male does not possess any visible inheritance factors, so the breeder does not know this until after the chicks have been hatched. It is claimed that the mating of a yellow female with a regular male produces the best offspring. In the yellow version, the male is pastel colored, though he retains his red rump, and the female is a creamy-yellow, an improvement on the original brown-green plumage. A yellow female, however, may end up with some red in the plumage after the molting. The English breeder Boosey has been breeding yellow Red Rumped Parrots since 1935, with incest taking place for at least six generations, without deterioration taking place in the form of lessened fertility and/or smaller body measurements. From this has originated a large tribe of yellow Red Rumped Parrots in Europe and elsewhere, which still attracts a lot of interest, as evidenced by the high prices that fanciers are prepared to pay for this variety."

In captivity cross-breeding has been established with other species of *Psephotus*, particularly the mulga parrot and the golden-shouldered parrot, as well as with a few rosellas (western and eastern rosellas) and with the mallee ringneck parrot (Forshaw, *Avic. Mag.,* 1962).

GENUS *NYMPHICUS*

The very well known cockatiel is the only representative belonging to this genus. Because of its crest, the little cere on the bill, and the cheek markings, one could place it in the cockatoo group, while its slender shape points to a close relationship with the rosella species. In fact, the cockatiel is somewhere between these two groups, though recently the tendency has been to place this beautiful bird closer to the rosellas. Formerly it was placed under the genus *Leptolophus* (*leptos* = delicate, *lophos* = crest or plume).

In Australia the cockatiel is very common, and I have seen it many times around Adelaide. Their graceful, somewhat curved flight is fast, and when seen as dark silhouettes against the sky they look a little like sparrow hawks. Their good flight capacities are due to their narrow, slender wings and the long tail that has three, four, or five extremely long central feathers. They also stand out because of their decorative crest.

I have noticed that they seem to like sitting on telegraph wires and other electric cables. They fly away as soon as they are approached, but soon circle around and return to their resting place. Practically every Sunday morning when I was on my way to church, taking a short cut through the parklands, I would come across a certain pair sitting on the telegraph wires (which are still strung across wooden poles). As soon as I would stop my car they would fly up, circle around, but very quickly return to their own little spot, glaring at me with crests raised! I rarely saw cockatiels on the ground. They live a nomadic existence, migrating to whatever regions offer the most food. Sometimes they can be seen in groups of several hundreds; a few decades ago they could be seen in flocks of a few thousands, according to Cayley.

Cockatiel (*Nymphicus hollandicus*)

Distribution: Australia: particularly in the interior, rarer along the coastal regions. Imported into Tasmania, though their wanderings have apparently also led them there.

Male: Grayish blue. Head and crest are yellow. Orange-yellow ear marking. White wing-coverts. Brown eyes; grayish blue bill; dark gray feet.

Female: Yellow on head and crest is less bright. Forehead, however, is brighter than that of the male. Dark ear marking. White wing-coverts are grayer.

Length: 30-33 cm (12-13 1/5 inches); wings 15-17 cm (6-6 4/5 inches); tail 14-17 cm (5 3/5-6 4/5 inches).

Particulars: This species makes excellent aviary birds, and even a beginner should have little difficulty in keeping a pair of them. Not only are they endowed with beautiful coloring, but with a noble crest and a fine build as well, making them great favorites among aviculturists. Houtenbos puts it very well in his book, *Ik kan vogels houden:*

"He spends the largest part of his day on the perches, with an occasional playful flight from one perch to another. It is amusing to watch him dribble across the floor of the aviary, with his crest straight up, and when he swings on his perches, all the while giving voice to their characteristic muttering. It's just as if he is mumbling to himself. Tolerance is, no doubt, his best virtue, both towards his keeper and all kinds of birds, both large and small. He is really very good natured, and would never do any harm to the other inhabitants.

Finally I would like to point out their high intelligence. My Cockatiels whistle the entire day, and the male, in particular, is capable of perfectly imitating all kinds of other bird sounds. All the while I was thinking that my Pekin nightingale was whistling his tune when I noticed that it was my Cockatiel which was singing so beautifully. When I go to feed my Cockatiel, he will bravely remain on his perch, even when I am just a few decimeters away from him. Finally, I am so close that his bill is near my forehead. If, at this close range, I then whistle to him—like exchanging so much gossip—he always answers me by whistling the same tune back to me."

They are also excellent breeders. The female lays four to seven eggs (26-30 x 17.5-24 mm), usually four or five, that take twenty days to hatch. The male sits on them during the day and the female at night. When the young are a good thirty days old they leave the nest but will continue to be fed by both parents for some time. The nesting box should measure 33 x 20 x 45 cm (13 x 8 x 18 inches) and an entrance hole diameter of 6 cm (2 2/5 inches). If we do not intervene they will continue to breed through the winter months as well.

Their menu should consist of the following: panicum millet, canary seed, oats, lots of greens (particularly when there are young in the nest), especially privet leaves, eggs, soaked seeds, bread, a few mealworms, ant-eggs, and slices of apples and carrots. The young, which resemble the female initially, often stick their little heads out of the nest, making a peeping "sissing" noise. It is a good idea to make the nesting box so the bird on the eggs will have its head at the height of the box opening; do not make the opening too high up. We should place a thick layer of sawdust on the bottom. In any case, do not use a nesting box where the entrance is too low, because cockatiels have the habit of leaving the nest when they are startled. When the bird on the nest has the opportunity to see everything that is happening around him or her, we should experience little trouble with deserted nests. We can only be sure of good breeding results when we house our birds in a roomy aviary by themselves. It speaks for itself that we should not disturb them when they are breeding; nest inspections, therefore, should be avoided unless we happen to have hand-tamed birds that are not bothered by our peeking into the "nursery." If our aviary has a good night shelter we can leave our cockatiels outside during the winter. Finally, I would like to point out that cockatiels often make outstanding foster parents for *Platycercus* species.

GENUS *EUNYMPHICUS*
Horned Parrakeet (*Eunymphicus cornutus*)

Distribution: New Caledonia and Ouvea (Loyalty Islands).

Male: Green with feathers on the head that are black with red tips. Area around the ear is a golden yellow. Flight feathers are blue. Yellow eyes with light yellow band; black-gray bill with light tip; slate colored feet. The bill is very sturdily built. Ornithologists recognize two subspecies of New Caledonia (*E.c. cornutus*) and the Loyalty Islands (*E.c. uvaeensis*).

Female: Less vivid in coloring than the male. The markings are also less obvious, and she is generally smaller of build. The crest is shorter.

Particulars: Fortunately, these beautiful birds have been offered for sale more frequently in recent years. They are quite expensive, but because they are so pleasant to have in the aviary and will breed well regularly fanciers are prepared to pay the price. They will easily earn back their original purchase price in one breeding season. In 1969 I had a pair that laid a clutch of four eggs (25.8-26.2x20.7-21.3 mm). Breeding time is March to October. The young left the nest after a month but continued to be fed by their parents for some time. See the cockatiel for food details. The young birds reached adult coloring after five weeks. For extra nutrition we can offer them peanuts, shelled hazelnuts, and walnuts. For a menu that is as varied as possible, feed the items suggested for *Platycercus*. Horned parrakeets are very affectionate toward their keepers; at least this has been my experience. They need to be brought indoors during the winter months into a moderately heated area.

GENUS *CYANORHAMPHUS*

Representatives belonging to this genus are rarely available for purchase. Ornithologists recognize six species that live in New Zealand, New Caledonia, and Tahiti, but their differences are very slight. Several are now extinct.

Red-fronted Parrakeet (*Cyanorhamphus novaezelandiae*)

Distribution: New Zealand and neighboring islands; New Caledonia.

Male and female: Red crown, forehead, ear marking, and rump. Green head, lighter on breast and belly. Flight feathers are dark green, edges light. Primaries blue. Dark green tail with black band. Blue-gray bill; orange-red eyes; dark gray feet.

Length: 23-26 cm (9 1/5-10 2/5 inches); wings 10-12.5 cm (4-5 inches); tail 11-13 cm (4 2/5-5 1/5 inches).

Particulars: These birds live in small groups, up to about eight pairs, and search on the ground for seeds and berries. The female lays three to seven eggs (25-26.2 x 21-23.3 mm) that take about twenty days to hatch. The male feeds the female during this period, and later they both feed the young, which fly out at 5 weeks. We know of a case where a pair reared 38 young in just one breeding season. We need to offer extra food to them during the breeding period, particularly ant-eggs and mealworms (25-30 per day!), also stale bread soaked in water or milk, universal food, and eggs.

In the wild, the breeding season takes place from November to the beginning of January; in the aviary, from March to late fall. Still, it is not advisable to allow them to breed constantly, because the next breeding season will be troubled with egg-binding or the birds may then be weakened to a point where they will not want to breed at all. There is yet a third possibility: the offspring from such continuous breeding efforts are often totally unsuitable for breeding. Consequently, we advise against more than three clutches per year. Nutritional needs must be completely met and weather conditions be good in order for our birds to achieve these successful breeding results. They must be brought indoors into a lightly heated area during the winter months.

One of the several subspecies is *Cyanorhamphus novaezelandiae cooki,* which lives on neighboring Norfolk island and differs from the typical red-fronted parrakeet only by the larger wings and a darker red coloring. *C.n. saissetti* lives on New Caledonia.

Yellow-fronted Parrakeet (*Cyanorhamphus auriceps*)

Distribution: New Zealand and neighboring islands.

Male and female: Coloring and markings are much like the previous species, except that the crown is a bright yellow and the breast is decorated with a blood-red marking. The primary flight feathers (2-5) are blue. Red-brown eyes; gray-brown beak; bright red-brown feet.

Length: 20-24.3 cm (8-9 4/5 inches); tail 10-11.5 cm (4-4 3/5 inches); wings 9.4-12 cm (3 4/5-4 4/5 inches).

Particulars: The somewhat smaller female lays 4-8 eggs (21.8-23 x 18.7-19 mm) in a well hidden nest in tree hollows, etc. Therefore it is a good idea to partially hide the nesting boxes (see cockatiel) so that the birds feel more at ease. This also applies to the previous species! Nutritional and breeding details parallel those of the previous species.

It is a pity that they are so rarely offered on the market. They should be brought indoors into a lightly heated area during the winter months. Unfortunately, we are not aware of any recent breeding results of birds kept in captivity.

GENUS *PLATYCERCUS*

No doubt this is the best known genus of the group, and its representatives are commonly held by aviary enthusiasts. The birds are characterized by their short, sturdy beak, the rounded, fairly sturdily built wings, and a gorgeous colorful coat. Many of the species are very common in Australia and are kept by many bird fanciers. All of the members of this genus are inhabitants of Australia and Tasmania; ornithologists recognize eight species.

Rosellas are found mostly in eastern and southern Australia; the well-known western rosella obviously lives in the west, while the northern rosella hails from the northern regions. The crimson rosella and the eastern rosella have a few subspecies that have been established according to geographical distribution. The populations of the most of these species are so large that ornithologists find that birds from a given area have slightly different coloring or perhaps a different marking than the same bird in an area a thousand miles away. The rosellas are known for their long, broad tails; the four center feathers are longer than the outermost feathers. They can also be identified by their shoulder and cheek markings, while the back feathers are scalloped and mostly black in color. They are extremely aggressive birds, particularly toward fellow species; needless to say, each pair will leave its group during the breeding season to rear their young alone. In the aviary we will need to supply them with nesting boxes and moist turf, wood mulch, etc.; their nests are made in tree hollows in the wild, and these, too, are always moist. The female lays four to nine eggs that take 18 days to hatch; this holds true for all the species. It is very difficult to determine their sex, which means, of course, that we should make the necessary arrangements with the seller so we may exchange one of our birds should they not form a pair. The western rosella, however, will not cause any problem in this area. Once young rosellas have become independent they will form their own group; they will never join a group that includes their parents. After twelve months the young birds are capable of starting their own families. A noteworthy point is the fact that rosella species that will keep each other's company in the wild will mate together both in captivity and in the wild. Consequently, it is supposed that the Adelaide rosella, as an example, is not actually a separate species but the result of cross-breeding. Personally I tend to doubt this, based on a lengthy study of the subject; we hope to come back to this in a future book.

Northern Rosella (*Platycercus venustus*)

Distribution: Australia, from Kimberly in northwestern Australia to the northern areas of Northern Territory; also on the islands of Melville and Bathurst (along the north coast).

Male and female: Crown and back of head brownish black to black. Cheeks are white with a broad sky-blue marking on the throat. Vague red glow on the forehead. Back and wings are black with broad yellow bands, giving a beautiful scalloped appearance. Yellow rump. Primary wing-coverts are light blue with black.

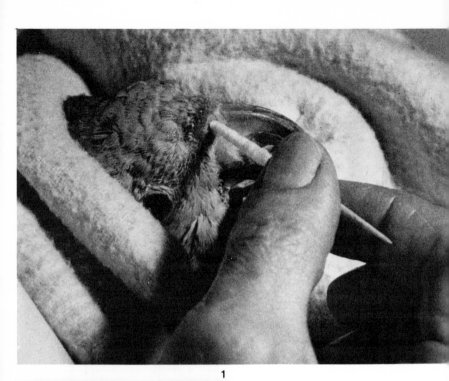

1. If your bird has a cold, keep its nostrils clean. 2. When cuttlebone is supplied, the bird will not be troubled with an overgrown beak. 3. A cage that does double duty, being able to be used as both a drying cage and a heated hospital cage.

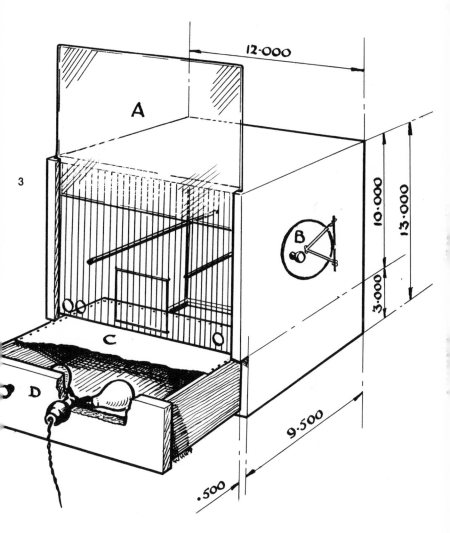

3

12·000

A

B

13·000

10·000

3·000

9·500

·500

C

D

A = Sliding glass door.
B = Spring-activated door.
C = Floor of drying chamber; serves as partition between bird and heat source.
D = Drawer housing heat source.

Flight feathers are darker and end in brownish green points. Tail blue-brown with dark blue edges, rimmed in white. Lower part of belly is red; underside of tail is blue with black point. Black eyes; light gray beak with blue point; black-brown feet. Several rosellas do not have the red on the forehead or have some yellow there instead. Other specimens may have red on the yellow, black-scalloped belly, or blue on the breast. These are not cases of impure races. Young birds differ from their parents by their less intense coloring. They achieve adult coloring after one year.

Length: 38 cm (15 1/5 inches); wings 14-15 cm (5 3/5-6 inches); tail 14.5-15 cm (6 inches).

Particulars: These birds live in pairs or in small groups (up to ten pairs). In the breeding period each pair goes off by themselves. They prefer the open woods, sometimes the edge of a mangrove swamp or creeks and rivers. Their flight is swift, and they can often be heard giving voice to their characteristic call, which is a fast "trinse" repeated three or four times. They feed on grass seeds and fruit. The northern rosella was first discovered in 1820 by the botanist Robert Brown. The female lays two or three white eggs, and the nest is made in a tree hollow. In captivity the breeding and molting times often coincide; the breeding season is in the winter, between December and February. Since molting and breeding may take place at the same time, it is important that we pay extra attention to their care. Strengthening foods, greens, fruit, a rich variety of seeds must never be missing in the menu. It is advisable to remove the other nesting boxes once the female has made her choice; otherwise it may happen that the female deserts her nest (often with two eggs in it) to start anew in another nesting box. The best breeding time, I think, is the end of January. Sawdust and mulched wood, preferably damp, should be placed in the nesting boxes before breeding has begun. During the breeding period it is most desirable for the birds to be offered plenty of greens (germinated seeds, lettuce, endives, chicory, chickweed, etc.), ant-eggs, and mealworms.

Western Rosella (*Platycercus icterotis*)
Distribution: Southwestern Australia, north to Moora and east to the Dundas area.

Male and female: Crown, throat, breast, and belly bright red. Flanks are mostly lighter red and have a sprinkling of yellow feathers among the red. Bright yellow cheeks. Back and rump green with black-scalloped coloring. Flight feathers are blue-black. The tail is green changing to blue toward the tip; underside of tail is sky-blue. The female is smaller in build and her coloring is less vivid. Many have some green feathers on the belly and head and smaller cheek markings. Young birds have green coloring with some red on the head. After 60-65 days the young birds will begin the molting period, after which it will be easier to distinguish between the sexes.

Length: 26-28 cm (10 2/5-11 1/5 inches); wing 12-14 cm (4 4/5-5 3/5 inches); tail 13-15 cm (5 1/5-6 inches).

Particulars: In the wild these birds live in pairs or in small groups (about ten pairs), and can do damage, particularly when they visit fruit orchards. In the aviary they need to have plenty of fruit (apples, pears, etc.). Once the female has laid her eggs, we should remove the other nesting boxes. In captivity she usually lays four to six eggs (22.8-23 x 18.7-19 mm) and five to seven in the wild. According to other breeders, and from my own experience, they prefer to have an aviary to themselves; ideal measurements are 3 meters long, 2 meters wide, and 1½ meters high (9 x 6 x 4½ feet). I have found these birds breed quite easily. Here again, we should place moist sawdust and mulched wood inside the nesting box.

Outside the breeding period they are very tolerant of fellow species and exotic birds, particularly young birds. Their song is quite pleasant. They can remain outside during the winter, providing they are sheltered from draft and rain; naturally a good night shelter is imperative. Personally I prefer to take them indoors for the winter (I even did this in Florida), so that we avoid the danger of having their toes freeze sooner or later. When they receive proper care they become very affectionate and will even take food from the aviary keeper's hand! If we are sure of the age of our birds, we can start having them breed at one year (thus before they have completed their adult coloring), although I personally prefer to wait until they are eighteen months of age, even if they do give a very sturdy and strong impression. Cross-breeding has taken place with the crimson rosella, the pale-headed rosella, and subspecies of the western rosella, but these should be avoided in order to preserve the purity of this bird's color and shape.

There are two subspecies. *Platycercus icterotis icterotis* is concentrated along the coast of southwestern Australia. The black feathers of the wings and back are rimmed in green; the head and underside are a beautiful red. Cheeks are deep yellow. The female has a green head and green underside with red shine. *Platycercus icterotis xanthogenys* is larger than the previous race and lives in the inland areas of southwestern Australia. The cheeks are light yellow; the back and wings are rimmed in red. Underside is red and yellow. Females are considerably brighter in color than the females of the prior races.

Eastern Rosella (*Platycercus eximius*)

Distribution: Australia; from southern Queensland to Victoria and the southeastern portions of South Australia (also west of Adelaide); also Tasmania.

Male and female: Breast, shoulders, neck, and head bright red. White cheek marking. Belly is yellow with green glow. Back is green with feathers edged in green-black, giving a scalloped appearance. Rump is green-yellow. Large flight feathers are blue. Tail is blue, with white band. Center tail feathers are green. Feathers under the tail are red. Brown eyes; gray-white beak; black-brown feet. The red on the female is less pronounced; her beak is smaller and the chest markings are grayish white. The coloring differences are not definite enough to determine the sex. The only certain indication of a female is the grayish brown feathers around the eyes, which the male lacks. Young birds have quite a lot of green on the neck.

Length: 30-32 cm (12-12 4/5 inches); wings 15-17 cm (6-6 4/5 inches); tail 16-18 cm (6 2/5-7 1/5 inches).

Particulars: Rosellas are known for being excellent breeders. Birds that are just one year of age can make a name for themselves for their good breeding abilities, even when they have finished their initial molting! The males can then be distinguished from the females because of the considerably greater amount of red feathers on their head. The female lays four to six eggs (in the wild as many as five to nine) that measure 26-28 x 22-22.8 mm. The male does not sit on them, but he will feed the young. The breeding period takes place from mid-February to May in captivity, September to January in the wild. They choose hollows in trees in which to build their nests, as well as tree stumps and openings in split-rail fences. When the young have been hatched, after about 24 days, they are fed by both parents. After about 30 days the fledglings leave the nest, and 10-15 months later they have achieved adult coloring. Independent birds should be separated from their parents; we should not use them for breeding until they are a year old or have achieved adult coloring.

In the wild these broad-tailed birds live in pairs or in large groups, particularly on open terrain spotted with some trees and bushes. They spend more time on the ground than in the trees and search for grass seeds, wild fruit, berries, and small insects. In cultivated areas they sometimes do considerable damage to orchards. Their whistling song is pleasant to hear.

The eastern rosella was first discovered in the vicinity of Rosehill (Parramatta), as Cayley says, ". . . in the early days of settlement; the name Rosella (originally Rosehiller) is derived from Rosehill" (named after the English founder, George Rose). A noteworthy fact is that in the wild, in the northeastern regions of New South Wales and the southestern areas of Queensland, this rosella occasionally mates with the pale-headed rosella.

At the beginning of this species' description I mentioned that its habitat includes Tasmania; this will need further explanation, because it is not entirely accurate. Strictly speaking, the Tasmanian variety is a subspecies, namely *Platycercus eximius diemensis*. There is, however, very little difference between the two other than that this subspecies is a few centimeters larger and the white cheeks continue further up the head. According to some ornithologists their coloring is brighter, but I did not find this to be true in all cases when I had the opportunity to study this bird in Australia and Tasmania. The rosella can also be found in New Zealand, but it is supposed that they were imported by fanciers many years ago.

In the Netherlands, the first breeding results were obtained in 1885. It enjoys popularity indeed. The English deportees kept them in cages and aviaries and found after some time that they were totally unsuitable as cage birds.

Breeding results can be obtained from a good pair year after year, providing their care is good. Dr. Groen quotes, as do a few English authors, 25-30 years of possible fertility!! So once you are in possession of a good pair, you can expect many years of pleasure. I purposely mention a "good" pair, because not every male will accept the first female that is presented to him—it would appear that he must have some choice in the matter. A female that is not to his liking will be aggressively chased. I like to quote Groen in this instance, because he is one of the best European breeders and experts on rosellas; he says the following in his book:

"Mating may cause problems because the males are sometimes aggressive towards the females, which are not always merely accepted. Initially, a couple may have some fights, of which the female gets the short end of the stick, and the aviary keeper will be forced to separate them. If we split up the pair and place them in adjoining aviaries for a couple of weeks, things may then work out when they are brought back together. When we choose two birds to form a pair, it is wise to place the male in the aviary of the female and not the other way around. If the female is accepted as a partner, we will be able to notice the growing amorousness of the male. The first signs are the spreading of the tail feathers and the shaking of the tail [horizontal movement of the spread tail]. Soon we can observe the male disappearing into one of the nesting boxes for the purpose of inspecting it. If the female follows his example and stays in the nesting box for some time, it is a sign that the choice has been made. During this period, many of the males have the habit of constantly chasing their female, who will be pursued to all the nooks and crannies of the aviary without any serious fights taking place. The feeding from the crop and the actual mating are signs that the first egg is practically on its way. The fancier with an experienced eye can tell when the female is close to the commencement of the laying of the eggs by observing that the lower abdomen is a little swollen. Towards evening the female will disappear into the nesting box, and the egg is usually laid in the early morning hours of the next day."

Rosellas enjoy an immense popularity with countless bird enthusiasts both here and in Europe, and of course in Australia. Any

366

kind of in-breeding, therefore, is totally unnecessary. They can be crossed with pale-headed rosellas, Adelaide rosellas, western rosellas, crimson rosellas, mallee ringneck parrots, or Port Lincoln parrots, red-rumped parrots, and various other bird species.

Platycercus eximius cecilae is a subspecies that can be found in Queensland and the northern part of New South Wales. This race differs from typical *Platycercus eximius* in that all the black feathers on the back are edged with deep yellow, which of course gives them a lovely appearance. The edges of typical *eximius* feathers are, after all, green in color. I also think the subspecies has more intense coloring, but the specimens that I have seen in the Netherlands were not as sharp in color as those I saw in the wild in Australia. Specimens kept in captivity in Australia were also sharper in coloring. The belly has a reddish glow. Under tail-coverts are a deep blue-green. The measurements are the same as in *eximius*.

It is a pity that this bird is not offered more regularly on the market, as they are excellent for breeding and rarely give any problems. They also become tame quite easily, even to the extent of taking food out of the keeper's hand. Fanciers with a limited budget will find this bird an excellent choice; birds that are just one year old will generally already produce good breeding results, and two clutches per season is not at all exceptional. They can also be of excellent service in the form of foster parents for more expensive rosella varieties. They can be crossed with other broad-tailed species, although the young are never as lovely and we would have to "cross them back" several times before some purity of race was again achieved. All in all, you can see that these birds make an ideal choice for keeping in a moderate-sized aviary, where they will live in peace and harmony with other birds. Even in the breeding period they do not cause very much trouble and will leave small exotic birds alone.

Crimson Rosella (*Platycercus elegans*)

Distribution: Australia: from Cairns and surrounding area in Queensland to Victoria and southeastern South Australia, as well as Kangaroo Island and King Island, with a similar race found on

Norfolk Island. The race that can be found in the northeastern part of Queensland is a few centimeters smaller and darker in coloring, but behavior patterns and way of life are the same as *Platycercus elegans*. The Norfolk Island race is scientifically known as *Platycercus elegans nigrescens* and is regularly offered for sale on the market as the crimson rosella. The differences are so slight that only ornithologists encumber themselves with them. The form that I saw in the area of the American River and along the Eleanor River on Kangaroo Island (which is the second largest island in Australia and is situated about ninety miles southwest of Adelaide, opposite the mouth of the Gulf of St. Vincent) has black "cloak" feathers and is scientifically known as *Platycercus elegans melanopterus*. The typical crimson rosella subspecies has been imported to Norfolk Island.

Male and female: Red. Throat, cheeks, and collar dark sky-blue. Wing-coverts and tail are blue. Flight feathers have a purplish blue glow. Cloak feathers are black, edged in red. The male has a slightly larger head and beak; young birds also tend to have this trait. Once the young are out of the nest, they generally look identical to the parents; sometimes they are a little greener in coloring. Eyes are dark brown; beak is grayish yellow, often ending in a black point. Feet are grayish brown.

Length: 32-36 cm (8-9 inches); wings 15-17 cm 6-6 4/5 inches); tail 14-17 cm (5 3/5-6 4/5 inches).

Particulars: In the wild these beautiful birds live in pairs or in groups concentrated in woody areas interspersed with fields and cultivated land. They spend a lot of time on the ground, searching for seeds from all kinds of grass types, etc., but also enjoy petals, juicy fruit (to the extent that orchard growers pursue and shoot them), and grain stalks. In contrast to the fact that they can do quite some damage to orchards, they also do a lot of good in consuming many destructive insects. Their song is a little shrill, but not altogether unpleasant, since it does include some musical notes. A noteworthy fact about their song is that it is imitated by the famous lyre bird.

These species are certainly not man-shy, as evidenced by the fact that I have occasionally seen them in the parks of Adelaide in South Australia. They are often seen around the foothills of Adelaide, too. On Kangaroo Island they often spend time in the cornfields, which of course is not very much appreciated by the farmers.

The birds use a cavity in a eucalyptus tree, in which the female lays four to six eggs, sometimes as much as seven (29 x 24 mm). The young are reared on seeds, corn, and caterpillars and other insects. Corn should not be missing from the menu in the aviary, as well as ant-eggs, whiteworms, and small mealworms.

This bird was first described in 1871 by Latham, who called it the "beautiful lory." In the aviary they have proved to be strong birds that can remain outside during the winter, providing, of course, ample shelter is offered them in the form of a well built night shelter. Since they are fairly aggressive by nature, it is best to give each couple their own reasonably sized aviary. Giving them a fresh supply daily of willow twigs will be a great help in soothing their enormous desire to gnaw. In order to avoid damage to the aviary, it is wise to protect the woodwork with metal strips. It is also a good idea to inspect the wire once a week.

Crimson rosellas are not known to be the best of breeders in captivity. We may find it helpful to make use of an incubator because the female does lay a lot of eggs. Cross-breeding has been accomplished with the eastern rosella, pale-headed rosella, the Port Lincoln parrot, the mallee ringneck parrot, and the rose-ringed parrakeet.

Pale-headed Rosella (*Platycercus adscitus*)

Distribution: Australia: northern and eastern parts of Queensland to the north of New South Wales, south to Sydney. Northern Queensland is the territory of a subspecies, *Platycercus adscitus amathusiae,* that is smaller and has blue cheek markings and a yellow marking on the breast.

Male and female: Yellow-white head; throat, breast and belly is sky blue, as are the flight feathers of the wings and tail. Under tail-coverts are red. Cloak feathers are black with yellow edges, giving a scalloped look. A black shoulder marking (usually larger in the male). White cheek markings, bottom edge bordered with blue. Grass-green rump with black markings. Male and female can generally not be distinguished from each other. Sometimes the female's coloring is less sharp than that of the male. The somewhat larger and flatter head of the male will give a clue as to his sex, but then only if we can make our comparisons with more birds. The male's eyes are larger, as is his neck. Dark brown eyes; gray-yellow bill; dark gray feet.

Length: 30-33 cm (12-13 1/5 inches); wings 14-16 cm (5 3/5-6 2/5 inches); tail 14-17 cm (5 3/5-6 4/5 inches).

Particulars: This bird was formerly known scientifically as *Platycercus palliceps;* its name was then changed to *adscitus,* which is Latin and means "new, take up, take over." In the wild these birds live in pairs or small groups and prefer open wooded areas. In the wild a good many of them have some red feathers on the head; these are probably cross-breeding results from the pale-headed and eastern rosellas. Their call is quite loud. Cayley says of their voices: "As is the case with other members of this group, the voices of the fledglings are so strong as to be almost startling."

The female lays four to six white eggs and chooses a cavity in a tree or tree trunk for her nest. Breeding takes place from September to part of December and nearly always after the rainy season; in other words, practically the entire year. In the aviary they start nesting box inspections as early as February. The breeding and rearing usually take place without a hitch; they also make good foster parents. It is a pity that imported birds often suffer from intestinal problems and that they are so difficult to acclimate. Once they have become accustomed to the local weather, though, they have a good constitution that can stand a little knock. Based on my personal experience, however, I feel it is wise to house the birds in a lightly heated area indoors during the winter months. When they are accustomed to weather and housing, they will easily rear two clutches per year. This species enjoys a lot of popularity in California, and breeders there have managed to obtain three clutches from one pair, without exhausting the female. Similar experiments will also be tried in Florida.

It would follow that birds that breed so easily also lend themselves well to cross-breeding. Consequently, cross-breeding results have been achieved with the following species: crimson rosella, eastern rosella, western rosella, northern rosella, Port Lincoln parrot, mallee ringneck parrot, red-rumped parrot, red-capped parrot, and blue bonnet parrot. Experience has shown that young birds in particular are very friendly and far more peaceful by nature than recently imported birds, which tend to scream incessantly, upsetting the entire aviary.

Lastly, I would like to mention that fledglings prefer a nesting box that has been covered with a layer of mulch, turf, etc. Before the eggs are laid, the female will busy herself, chewing the wood chips, etc. into the right shape, and getting the nest into ship-shape. Once she has completed this task, you can expect the first egg within just a few days.

Adelaide Rosella (*Platycercus adelaidae*)

Distribution: South Australia (Mount Lofty and the Flinders Ranges).

Male and female: It is not a simple matter to prepare a definitive color description of this species, because I have seldom seen specimens that were uniformly colored and marked. Many birds look a great deal like the crimson rosella due to their intensive red colors; yet others have so much yellow in their plumage that they are difficult to distinguish from the yellow rosella, yet to be discussed. Of course a few details are not as fluctuating. These are: the main color is red; the head has some dark shadows; the cheeks and throat are blue; and the back is pinkish red, with black feathers that are margined in yellow-red. The shoulders are black; large flight feathers are blue; and the rump is red. The tail is blue, the central tail feathers having a green glow. Cloak feathers are margined in pale red in the male, while in the female the margins are even narrower and are pinkish red to yellowish green; but even these colors do not give us any certainty with regard to sex. The larger and flatter head of the male, however, does offer us a solution, although this is certainly not always correct. Young birds are bluish green and achieve adult coloring after twelve months.

Length: 30-35 cm (12-14 inches); wings 15-17 cm (6-6 4/5 inches); tail 15-17 cm (6-6 4/5 inches).

Particulars: This infrequently kept bird has kept ornithologists guessing for some time. It is still not certain whether this bird is a separate species or the result of cross-breeding that managed to survive and is now quite plentiful. According to Keast, Condon, and others, the Adelaide rosella would be a variety of crimson rosella (*Platycercus elegans adelaidae*). This was based on the fact that the crimson rosella has four subspecies or varieties as follows: the subspecies from Queensland that is darker in color; the specimens we are treating here as the Adelaide rosella, which are quite variable in coloring; the birds from New South Wales that have a considerably less bright plumage; and finally, the Kangaroo Island variety. If we believe other ornithologists, then it would have been a crossing between the crimson rosella and the yellow rosella that produced this variety. It is indeed true that resultant birds from such a crossing look almost identical (in fact, I do believe entirely identical) to the Adelaide rosella. They live in small groups or in pairs in open wooded areas.

Mathews recognizes yet another form, namely *Platycercus elegans subadelaidae.* There is only a small amount of red that shines through on the breast of this bird, and the back feathers are black and margined with bright yellow; in other words, there is no longer any red present on this variety. The belly, too, has no red, but is pure yellow in color. Naturally, aviculturists keep and breed all of the varieties without distinction, which I feel is a shame.

Yellow Rosella (*Platycercus flaveolus*)

Distribution: Australia: in the valleys of the Lachlan, Murrumbidgee, and Darling Rivers in New South Wales as well as the valley of the Murray River in New South Wales, Victoria, and South Australia.

Male and female: Yellow head, with a little red on the forehead and around the eyes. Blue cheeks. Underside of body and rump are yellow. Under tail-coverts are yellow; underside of tail also a greenish yellow. Cloak feathers are black, as are the center feathers of the wing-coverts, and these are margined in yellow. Black shoulders. Here again, the difference in the size of the head is the only indication with regard to sex. The young achieve adult coloring after one year; before that there is white mixed in with the yellow coloring. Brown eyes; grayish yellow bill; grayish brown feet.

Length: 32-36 cm (8-9 inches); wings 14-17 cm (5 3/5-6 4/5 inches); tail 14-17 cm (5 3/5-6 4/5 inches).

Particulars: It is a pity that these birds are not kept by more fanciers. Personally, I feel they deserve a great deal more attention than they presently draw. They are good breeders—at least that was my experience in Florida. They live in pairs or small groups in immediate proximity to water and open terrain. They spend much of their time on the ground, where they search for seeds and small insects. If they are startled, they hide in the low shrubbery. The female lays four to five white eggs (24 x 20 mm) in the cavity of a tree.

These birds are enjoying an immense popularity in California (and also with some Florida breeders), where they have been cross-bred with the northern rosella. When one considers that bird's size, this is indeed quite an achievement. The yellow rosella is certainly a breed that lends itself to these experiments, as evidenced by the cross-breeding successes that have been achieved through the years, such as with the Adelaide rosella, the eastern rosella, the crimson rosella, the mallee ringneck parrot, the Port Lincoln parrot and the red-rumped parrot; quite possibly this list is not even complete.

Green Rosella (*Platycercus caledonicus*)

Distribution: Tasmania and the islands in the Bass Strait.

Male and female: Golden yellow; yellow head with brown shadow; blue cheek markings; red lores and forehead. Wings edged in blue; underside of tail is also blue. Cloak feathers are black, edged in green. Olive-green rump. Female is a little smaller in build and has a green tint on the yellow coloring. There is also less red on the forehead, but this is difficult to determine without the presence of other birds with which comparisons can be made. The head and bill of the male are definitely larger and more sturdily built. Young birds are primarily green, and it often takes as much as two years before they have completed the coloring process. Brown eyes; yellow-gray bill; grayish brown feet.

Length: 32-36 cm (8-9 inches); wings 14-17 cm (5 3/5-6 4/5 inches); tail 14-17 cm (5 3/5-6 4/5 inches).

Particulars: The scientific name is very confusing, since *caledonicus* indicates New Caledonia, where the species is *not* found. They live on Tasmania and the islands of the Bass Strait in pairs or small groups, preferably in open wooded country and barren areas, but also in thick woods and even orchards, where they can be a real pest. They live mainly on the blossoms of the eucalyptus tree and on grass and other plant seeds that they find on the ground. They can also be found in villages and small towns, and I got the impression when studying them at close range that they are not shy of being near man and civilization. Their call sounds like "kussick, kussick." This bird is not protected by law. Many of them are bred by the people of Tasmania and South Australia.

The female lays four to six white eggs (24x20 mm), and in the wild as many as six to nine. It is a shame that they are not bred more often here, as experience has shown that they breed quite readily, even twice a year if given proper care. Cross-breeding has taken place several times with the eastern rosella. The green rosella can also be cross-bred with the Adelaide rosella, the Port Lincoln parrot, and the mallee ringneck parrot. Here again, I would like to point out that cross-breeding is a practice that is better avoided, as it does nothing to enhance race purity.

GENUS *BARNARDIUS*

When John Gould published his books on Australian birds, he included in the genus *Platycercus* some four species that had been studied at length by the eighteenth century English biologist Edward Barnard (London) and were then reclassified into a separate genus. It is also strange that Peters, in a fairly recent listing of birds of the world, makes this same mistake. In Cayley's latest edition, these birds are identified with their "new" scientific name, while Immelmann of course uses this same, better classification in his excellent book *Die australischen Plattschweifsittiche* (A. Ziemsen Verlag, Wittenberg, Lutherstadt DDR), following Condon, who based this classification change on the difference in the build of the skull as well as the striking difference in coloring and the clearly visible neck-ring.

The coloring differences in these birds are great enough that this alone should be reason enough to place them in a separate genus. Here are a few coloring differences: specimens belonging to *Barnardius* all have a clearly visible yellow neck-ring; they lack the black cloak marking and shoulder marking; the cheeks are not as clearly defined; the beak is larger; and the tail is longer and more slender than that of the rosellas, which stand out for their flat tails.

When extended proper care, the *Barnardius* group will breed well. For further particulars, please refer to the genus *Platycercus* and the text regarding the eastern rosella. The general remarks, especially those regarding care and breeding, made in the first part of this book, should also be of service.

Mallee Ringneck Parrot (*Barnardius barnardi*)

Distribution: Interior of southern Queensland, western New South Wales, northwestern Victoria, and eastern part of South Australia, west to the York Peninsula.

Male and female: Blue-green; green dominates. Darker on the breast, more yellowish on the division of breast and belly. Dark green on the back. Green-blue cloak; the green on rump and upper tail-coverts is edged in blue. A lot of brownish green tint on the head. Clearly visible red band on the forehead. Wing curve is blue and green-blue underneath the tail. Yellow neck-ring; bluish green on throat. The female is not as sharp in markings and has a smaller head and bill. After twelve months, the young achieve adult coloring.

Length: 32-34 cm (8-8 3/5 inches); wings 16-18 cm (6 2/5-7 1/5 inches); tail 17-19 cm (6 4/5-7 3/5 inches).

Particulars: In the wild these birds live in pairs or together in small groups of about eight to ten pairs. They prefer wooded country near large rivers and spend most of the day on the ground searching for seeds, small insects, etc. They consider eucalyptus buds a treat and will give voice to some rambunctious screeching while eating them. The female lays four to five white eggs in the cavity of a tree.

Another variety is *Barnardius barnardi whitei,* which lives in South Australia (around Lake Eyre) and is darker in coloring, smaller in build, and has the divisional band between breast and belly orange instead of yellow. Then there is the blue variety, known as *Barnardius barnardi crommelinae.* Both varieties are seldom seen in Europe, though of course they are common enough with Australian breeders. Beautiful specimens can be seen in the Adelaide Zoo, while the Leiden Museum of Natural History has several stuffed specimens staged in beautiful natural settings.

Entirely unknown in Europe is *Barnardius barnardi macgillivrayi* (named after A.S. MacGillivray, Leilavale Stn., Cloncurry, Queensland), which barely shows any difference from the mallee ringneck parrot. It is, however, smaller, and lacks the green on the neck and on the back of the head as well as the red on the forehead. The head is more of a bluish green. There is no yellow in the wings. The chin is dark blue. They are very rare and live in pairs or in small groups in the interior of northwestern Queensland around Cloncurry.

Port Lincoln Parrot (*Barnardius zonarius*)

Distribution: Northwestern and central-west Australia, central Australia, and the interior of South Australia to Lake Eyre, the Flinders Ranges, and Spencer Gulf.

Male and female: Black head with blue feathers at the sides of the neck. Dark green breast, the feathers having light edges, giving a scalloped appearance. Broad yellow belly marking that extends to the under tail-coverts. Under tail-coverts and part of lower belly are green. Yellow neck-ring. Tail edged in light blue. Brown eyes; grayish white bill; brown gray feet. Young birds have a brownish black head.

Length: 34-37 cm (13 3/5-14 4/5 inches); wings 17-19 cm (6 4/5-7 3/5 inches); tail 18-20 cm (7 1/5-8 inches).

Particulars: This bird lives in pairs or small groups in open wooded areas, open terrain profuse with shrubbery, and along the water's edge. Their numbers have decreased over the last hundred years, particularly due to the fact that many of them are shot by farmers because of the destruction they wreak in orchards and cornfields. Since their territory covers an enormous area, it is unlikely that they will become extinct, though some caution should be exercised. Studies have made it clear that their number still continues to drop, if not by any large figures.

In Western Australia there is a subspecies known as *Barnardius zonarius occidentalis.* This bird is considerably smaller in build and the coloring is less vivid; the green in the wings, in particular, is rather vague. The head is grayish black. Breeding is a simple matter with them.

Barnardius zonarius semitorquatus (the "twenty-eight" parrot) is another subspecies. This bird is much larger than the typical Port Lincoln parrot and brighter in coloring. The neck-ring is larger and a brighter yellow. The cloak feathers are yellow. There is a red band on the forehead. The male's beak is larger than that of the female. This bird inhabits the southwestern regions of Australia north to Perth and east to Albany. There is variety of this bird known as the *Barnardius zonarius semitorquatus "dundasi,"* that lives in the neighborhood of Lake Dundas (southwestern Australia). They live in pairs or in large groups in open woods and bushy areas. They do considerable damage to fruit orchards and are, as a consequence, often shot down by the farmers; they also like to eat rye. They are known as excellent cage birds in Australia.

Barnardius occidentalis from central Australia (from the Murchison River to the Fortescue River) is much smaller than the previously mentioned species. Finally there is *Barnardius myrtae,* which can be found in the northern areas of South Australia to the southern regions of Northern Territory. This bird looks a great deal like the Port Lincoln parrot but has more green on the back with a clearly visible yellow glow. All races adhere to Gloger's law: specifically, all bird races which live near the coast where there is a lot of humidity have more green in their plumage, so the melanism is stronger with these birds than those living inland, where the melanism becomes weaker and the green is replaced by yellow.

GENUS *NEOPSEPHOTUS* (or subgenus of *Neophema*)

Although the majority of ornithologists include Bourke's parrot under the genus *Neophema,* I believe in following von Boetticher that this species should be placed in another genus, since its build, way of life, and coloring vary markedly from the fairly uniform group of *Neophema* representatives. In addition, we would point out that there are no cross-breeding results established with rosellas or other species, such as is also the case with the budgerigar and cockatiel, so that it is perfectly justified to speak of a separate genus.

Bourke's Parrot *(Neophema bourkii* or *Neopsephotus bourkii)*

Distribution: From southwestern Queensland and deep into the western portion of New South Wales through central Australia to the northernmost portion of South Australia and a few areas in the inland of Western Australia.

Male and female: Pink; black-brown scalloping. Crown, neck, back, wings, and tail are auburn. Edge of wing is blue, as is the underside of the tail feathers. Blue-white eye marking. Wing feathers have a white band. Outermost tail feathers are blue-white. Female has a rounder head and usually lacks most of the blue coloring above the beak. After nine, sometimes eight, months the young achieve adult coloring, but until that time it is virtually impossible to sex them. Only the rounder heads of the females may be an indication, but not a certainty. Eyes are brown; beak is a shiny black; light brown feet.

Length: 21-22 cm (8 2/5-8 4/5 inches); wings 10-12 cm (4-4 4/5 inches); tail 10-11 cm (4-4 2/5 inches).

Particulars: Recently imported birds should not be placed in an outside aviary for five months; they must first become accustomed to our climate. Warmth is a very important requirement for these birds, so they must not be allowed to stay outside during the winter months for the first year if we want to avoid dead or sick birds!

This species was named after Sir Richard Bourke, who was governor of New South Wales from 1831 to 1837. *Neophema* is Greek and means: *neos* = new; *pheme* = voice; their voice is indeed very pleasant to the ear.

If we provide our Bourke's parrots with a good menu, good housing, and offer a little extra treat once in a while, I can guarantee that these birds will live a long life. I have known cases where they lived for twelve years and longer in good health in an aviary. Since in the wild they feed mainly on seeds (grass seeds and seeds from the acacia and spinifex, which are preferably sought in the vicinity of water), we should offer them a variety of seeds in the aviary, even though this is often a problem because they do not readily become accustomed to the seeds we offer them. (More elaborate details can be found in *De Vogelgids,* 15th year, No. 174, page 10-11, in which I wrote an article, "Bourke's Parrots are threatened with extinction.") It is obviously much simpler to purchase specimens that have been locally bred, making sure, of course, that they are not related. Hard boiled eggs and oven-dried bread will provide some change for them, while plenty of greens and fresh buds and twigs should not be left out. Once imported birds have become accustomed to local climate and the seed menu (panicum millet, oats, hemp, canary seed, weed, and grass seeds) they can be placed in the outside aviary (mid-June).

The female will start to breed quickly, particularly when she has become accustomed to the weather and can stay outdoors during the winter without the danger of becoming ill. In February she will lay three to seven eggs (17.8-18x15.6-16 mm), although usually four or five. She alone will sit on the eggs for about twenty days. The male will feed her during this time, and later the young as well. Each season a couple can rear three to four clutches. The young are reared on canary nestling food and the extra nutritional foods mentioned earlier. Ant-eggs, mealworms, soaked rice, corn, bread soaked in milk, and sometimes fruit are welcome, too. When given good care, owners have little trouble in keeping these birds healthy and lively and encouraging them to breed.

In the wild they are most active toward evening; early in the morning, before the sun has barely risen, they are already busy searching for food. In the aviary they will be busiest in the early morning and in the evening without bothering any other aviary inhabitants. Just before and during the breeding period, they will also be busy during the day. The male, in particular, will be very active when the female is sitting on the eggs. He will constantly fly back and forth in the aviary, nervously sitting on top of the nesting box and regularly popping into the box to make sure everything is still in order. The female also willingly allows checking by the bird breeder, though we should not overdo this of course. Young birds that are flying out of the nest are quite wild. We should keep a close watch on them because they may very well injure themselves flying against the wire or walls. We can alleviate this problem by placing plants against the walls and sticking some green twigs through the wire roof, etc., which will alert them to the obstacles. Bourke's parrots make excellent foster parents for fellow species as well as for species belonging to the genus *Psephotus*.

Index

Page numbers set in *italic* type refer to illustrations.